I0410600

S. Hrg. 114–69

DEEPENING POLITICAL AND ECONOMIC CRISIS IN VENEZUELA: IMPLICATIONS FOR U.S. INTERESTS AND THE WESTERN HEMISPHERE

HEARING

BEFORE THE

SUBCOMMITTEE ON WESTERN HEMISPHERE TRANSNATIONAL CRIME, CIVILIAN SECURITY, DEMOCRACY, HUMAN RIGHTS, AND GLOBAL WOMEN'S ISSUES

OF THE

COMMITTEE ON FOREIGN RELATIONS UNITED STATES SENATE

ONE HUNDRED FOURTEENTH CONGRESS

FIRST SESSION

MARCH 17, 2015

Printed for the use of the Committee on Foreign Relations

Available via the World Wide Web: http://www.gpo.gov/fdsys/

U.S. GOVERNMENT PUBLISHING OFFICE

96–257 PDF   WASHINGTON : 2015

For sale by the Superintendent of Documents, U.S. Government Publishing Office
Internet: bookstore.gpo.gov   Phone: toll free (866) 512–1800; DC area (202) 512–1800
Fax: (202) 512–2104   Mail: Stop IDCC, Washington, DC 20402–0001

COMMITTEE ON FOREIGN RELATIONS

BOB CORKER, TENNESSE, *Chairman*

JAMES E. RISCH, Idaho	ROBERT MENENDEZ, New Jersey
MARCO RUBIO, Florida	BARBARA BOXER, California
RON JOHNSON, Wisconsin	BENJAMIN L. CARDIN, Maryland
JEFF FLAKE, Arizona	JEANNE SHAHEEN, New Hampshire
CORY GARDNER, Colorado	CHRISTOPHER A. COONS, Delaware
DAVID PERDUE, Georgia	TOM UDALL, New Mexico
JOHNNY ISAKSON, Georgia	CHRISTOPHER MURPHY, Connecticut
RAND PAUL, Kentucky	TIM KAINE, Virginia
JOHN BARRASSO, Wyoming	EDWARD J. MARKEY, Massachusetts

LESTER E. MUNSON III, *Staff Director*
JODI B. HERMAN, *Democratic Staff Director*

SUBCOMMITTEE ON WESTERN HEMISPHERE TRANSNATIONAL CRIME, CIVILIAN SECURITY, DEMOCRACY, HUMAN RIGHTS, AND GLOBAL WOMEN'S ISSUES

MARCO RUBIO, Florida, *Chairman*

JEFF FLAKE, Arizona	BARBARA BOXER, California
CORY GARDNER, Colorado	TOM UDALL, New Mexico
DAVID PERDUE, Georgia	TIM KAINE, Virginia
JOHNNY ISAKSON, Georgia	EDWARD J. MARKEY, Massachusetts

(II)

CONTENTS

DEEPENING POLITICAL AND ECONOMIC CRISIS IN VENEZUELA: IMPLICATIONS FOR U.S. INTERESTS AND THE WESTERN HEMISPHERE

TUESDAY, MARCH 17, 2015

U.S. SENATE, SUBCOMMITTEE ON WESTERN HEMISPHERE,
TRANSNATIONAL CRIME, CIVILIAN SECURITY, DEMOC-
RACY, HUMAN RIGHTS, AND GLOBAL WOMEN'S ISSUES,
COMMITTEE ON FOREIGN RELATIONS,

Washington, DC.

The subcommittee met, pursuant to notice, at 10:07 a.m., in room SD–419, Dirksen Senate Office Building, Hon. Marco Rubio (chairman of the subcommittee) presiding.

Present: Senators Rubio, Flake, Gardner, Perdue, Isakson, Boxer, Menendez, Udall, Kaine, and Markey.

OPENING STATEMENT OF HON. MARCO RUBIO, U.S. SENATOR FROM FLORIDA

Senator RUBIO. The committee will come to order. To start this hearing, the Subcommittee on the Western Hemisphere, Transnational Crime, Civilian Security, Democracy, Human Rights, and Global Women's Issues will come to order, as I said.

This hearing is titled ''The Deepening Political and Economic Crisis in Venezuela: Implications for U.S. Interests and the Western Hemisphere.''

I would like to begin by welcoming Mr. Alex Lee, who is the Deputy Assistant Secretary of State for South America and Cuba, and Mr. John E. Smith, the Acting Director of Office of Foreign Assets Control.

We had invited Assistant Secretary of State Roberta Jacobson to participate. We were informed that she is in Havana today so she will not be available. So we appreciate you being here, Mr. Lee.

So with vast oil reserves, Venezuela is one of the richest countries in Latin America, and the Venezuelan people are intelligent, they are well educated, they are hardworking people. The evidence of this can be found in my home State in Miami and in Doral and in Weston, FL, where a vibrant Venezuelan community has helped build quality and vibrant communities.

And Venezuela is also the cradle of democracy in South America. And that is why it is so tragic that Venezuela has turned into a social, political, and economic disaster.

The reason for this is simple. Because today that nation is increasingly in the iron grip of corrupt and incompetent leaders. A rich country suffering from a massive and growing shortage of food, medicine, and basic goods to the point where Maduro has had to order supermarkets to install fingerprint scanners to enforce food rations. Venezuela has an inflation rate of over 60 percent, among the highest in the world. Price controls in Venezuela have led to massive shortages of medicine and medical equipment, has forced hospitals to suspend cancer treatments and all but emergency surgical procedures. Shortages of spare parts have grounded much of the bus and truck fleet, and many airlines have stopped flying to Venezuela altogether.

The government, by the way, has also defaulted on several large debts. Back when they were facing elections in 2012 and 2013, they authorized more imports than they could afford, but when the bills came due, they stopped paying them, building up tens of billions of dollars' worth of debt. The result is that Venezuelan bonds are treated as among the riskiest in the world, demanding premiums that are twice those of Bolivia, four times those of Nigeria, and 13 times those of Mexico or Chile.

It is the incompetence of Nicolas Maduro and his predecessor, Hugo Chavez, that have left Venezuela in the position that it finds itself in. But instead of seeking out reforms to improve these conditions, the response of the Maduro regime has been to crack down on dissent, erode democracy, and violently violate the human rights of their own people.

Here is just a brief recap of steps Maduro and his cronies have taken to strengthen their grip on power.

In April 2013, the main opposition TV network, Globovision, was forced to sell to a pro-government owner.

In July 2013, pro-government businessmen bought Cadena Capriles, the owner of the largest daily in Venezuela, Ultimas Noticias.

In August 2013, the most corrupt man in Venezuela—and that is one heck of a title—Mr. Diosdado Cabello, the National Assembly President, used a simple majority vote instead of the required two-thirds vote to suspend an opposition deputy from office, paving the way for a series of votes to grant Maduro decree powers.

In September 2013 Maduro closes Voz de Orinoco, a radio station. He closed it for, ''calling for rebellion.''

In October 2013, Maduro restricts bulk paper imports to opposition newspapers, making it harder for them to go to print.

In February 2014, security officials, working with armed pro-government thugs, confront, beat, and even kill anti-Maduro protestors.

That same month, the National Telecommunications Commission prohibits local TV and radio from covering antigovernment protests.

In May 2014, the Maduro government begins to routinely block Web sites that are critical of the regime.

In July 2014, a Spanish investor group close to Maduro buys El Universal, one of the nation's flagship daily newspapers, and immediately the content of that newspaper changes to one of supportive of Maduro.

In August 2014, the government begins proceedings against Radio Caracas, and it suspends an opposition radio show from broadcasting.

This is just a small sampling of the antidemocratic moves and the violent moves taken by this regime just in the last year and a half.

Now, faced with these long string of human rights violations and the fact that many of these violators and the people who enable them have strong economic links to the United States and in particular south Florida, late last year Congress passed and the President signed a law allowing the United States to deny visas and freeze the assets of human rights violators in Venezuela. And last week, the President applied these sanctions against several human rights violators.

These sanctions are not against the Government of Venezuela. These sanctions are not against the people of Venezuela, nor do they aim to deny the people of Venezuela anything. These sanctions, that the President has imposed, deny known human rights violators the chance to use the money they have stolen from the people of Venezuela to enjoy luxuries here in the United States. These sanctions also deny human rights violators the chance to travel freely to the United States.

Faced with an economic catastrophe and dwindling public support, Nicolas Maduro has tried to use these sanctions as a way to deflect from these problems and rally people around anti-Americanism and nationalism. He has gone as far as to absurdly claim that the United States is preparing an invasion of Venezuela, and he has tried to place the opposition in a position of either supporting him or being labeled as traitors.

So let me be very clear. The future of Venezuela belongs to the people of Venezuela to decide via free and fair elections. The United States has no interest and no plans of imposing or encouraging what direction a free people of Venezuela freely choose. The purpose of these sanctions is only this: to deny corrupt officials and human rights violators the opportunity to buy homes, make investments, and vacation in the United States with the money they have stolen from the people of Venezuela.

Nevertheless, we can expect to see more of these theatrics from Nicolas Maduro in the days and weeks to come. In fact, we have just received word that he is shopping around an open letter to the American people to be published any day now in some major American media outlet or various media outlets, encouraging the American people to stand up to their elected officials and ask them to stop picking on him. By the way, in the same letter, he accuses the United States of being involved in a 2002 coup plot in Venezuela, another absurd claim.

This past weekend he asked for and was given absolute power once again by the National Assembly. This grab for power through decree powers that were given to him—you can expect to see more of this because the declining economy and falling oil prices has cut into his ability to buy support. Here are some of the things we expect to see.

Unable to find credible evidence of coup plots between the opposition and U.S. diplomats, I expect and predict that soon you will see them produce fabricated evidence of coup plotting. You will see clandestine assassination of opposition figures, and you may even see Maduro and his cronies try to move up this year's legislative elections to capitalize on this nationalism before the popularity of his government fades even more.

But no amount of repression or theatrics will solve or cover up the disaster that he has brought upon the people of Venezuela. Food seized from private stores rot in warehouses because of their incompetence. Maduro and his cronies continue to manipulate currency to make money for themselves. Maduro and his cronies will continue to force those doing business with the government to use companies where they control the subcontractors. And at some point this year, we may even see the gas subsidies, long provided by the government, either altered or removed altogether.

And we will also continue to see human rights violations. The Defense Minister Vladimir, Padrino Lopez, has authorized the use of force against peaceful demonstrators, which has led to the murder of a 14-year-old boy. We will see more arrests like the recent one of the elected Mayor of Caracas, Antonio Ledezma, who was arrested last month. And sadly, we will see more deaths such as one when opposition leader Rodolfo Gonzalez took his own life when faced with the Maduro decision to move the dissident leader to a cell block of common criminals.

It is also worth noting some other aspects of this regime.

First, the Cuban dictatorship has penetrated every aspect of the Venezuelan Government. We will get into that today.

Second, Maduro has opened the door to closer military relations with Iran, Russia, and China. In fact, the Venezuelan military is currently conducting exercises with visiting Russian troops and equipment.

Third, the Maduro regime continues to harbor vast elements of the FARC within Venezuelan territory, offering this terrorist group sanctuary and protection.

And fourth, along with Cuba, Maduro continues to aid populist anti-American elements throughout Central and South America.

The people of Venezuela deserve better than this, and while the direction of their future belongs to them, we will be a strong voice in firm support of their aspirations for a better country and a better life. And we will not allow those who are violating their rights and denying them this better future the chance to come to Doral or Weston or to Miami or CocoPlum and enjoy life with the money they have stolen from their own people.

With that, I would like to thank and recognize our ranking member, Senator Boxer, and I look forward to continuing to work with you on these important issues.

STATEMENT OF HON. BARBARA BOXER,
U.S. SENATOR FROM CALIFORNIA

Senator BOXER. Thank you so much for holding this really important and very timely hearing. And I also would like to thank our witnesses for participating.

In February 2014, thousands of Venezuelans took to the streets to protest against the administration of President Nicolas Maduro and were met with a brutal crackdown by government security forces and armed pro-government gangs.

Last month marked the 1-year anniversary of these widespread antigovernment demonstrations, which lasted nearly 4 months and left more than 40 people dead.

Tragically, the grievances voiced by protestors—a failing economy, chronic shortages of consumer goods, and high levels of crime, violence, and corruption—have certainly not been addressed. In fact, the political and economic situation in Venezuela has continued to deteriorate over the past year.

According to official figures, Venezuela's economy shrank 2.8 percent in 2014 and inflation rose to 64 percent, the highest rate in Latin America. Venezuela's murder rate is the second-highest in the world behind Honduras. And Transparency International ranks Venezuela as the most corrupt country in Latin America.

The Maduro government continues its brutal repression of dissent by systematically targeting opposition figures, human rights defenders, journalists, and civil society activists for violence, harassment, intimidation, and other human rights abuses. Just last month, the mayor of Caracas was arrested and jailed for allegedly, ''conspiring to organize and carry out violent acts against the government,'' and a 14-year-old boy was shot in the head and killed by a police officer during an antigovernment protest.

In response to the deepening crisis in Venezuela, Congress unanimously enacted the Venezuela Defense of Human Rights and Civil Society Act of 2014, which President Obama signed into law in December. This very important law requires the President to impose sanctions on individuals or entities involved in serious human rights violations against antigovernment protestors, or on those who have ordered the arrest or prosecution of individuals for their legitimate exercise of freedom of expression or assembly. I applaud President Obama's decision to implement this law by sanctioning seven Venezuelan officials involved in human rights abuses and public corruption, and I encourage him to continue that crackdown.

The United States has an obligation to shine a bright light on the abuses being committed against the people of Venezuela, and the President's action sends a strong message to the people there and the government that we will not stay silent in the face of violence, corruption, and the suppression of the fundamental rights and freedoms of the Venezuelan people.

But it is also important to make clear that these sanctions directly target the perpetrators of abuses. They do not target the people of Venezuela. And as our chairman said, that is critical. We want to hurt the people who are causing all this hurt, not the ordinary people who are simply trying to survive.

Today's hearing will be an important opportunity to examine the United States policy toward Venezuela and the role of sanctions in addressing the current economic and political crisis there. It will also help us chart a path forward in support of the people of Venezuela and their aspirations; their aspirations that are just like all people, a longing to be truly free and truly democratic.

Thank you very much, Mr. Chairman.

Senator RUBIO. Thank you.

The ranking member of the Foreign Relations Committee and someone who spends a tremendous amount of time on Western Hemisphere issues is here with us today, and I would like to recognize him for some comments.

STATEMENT OF HON. ROBERT MENENDEZ, U.S. SENATOR FROM NEW JERSEY

Senator MENENDEZ. Thank you, Mr. Chairman. Thank you and the ranking member for holding what I think is an incredibly important hearing. There are many challenges in the world that distract or diversify our attention, but this one in our own hemisphere is incredibly important.

Last may, after 40 deaths, more than 50 documented cases of torture, high profile political persecutions, and thousands of arbitrary and unlawful detentions by the Venezuelan Government, this committee met to review the shocking pattern of systematic human rights violations by the Maduro government, its security forces, and its judicial system which continues today and has only gotten worse.

Venezuela is awash in a culture of gross impunity at every level. Checks and balances on Executive power have completely eroded. There is no accountability for the crimes against Venezuelan citizens by an out-of-control regime.

It should come as no surprise, as Venezuela's fiscal and economic crisis has deepened, that the Maduro government is radicalizing its tactics. Last month, the Minister of Defense, Padrino Lopez, signed a decree authorizing security forces to use lethal force—lethal force—against civilians, and with that decree came the tragic death of 14-year-old Kluiverth Roa, who was shot in the head by the national police.

We saw, as has been said here, the elected mayor of Caracas, Antonio Ledezma, forcefully removed from this office and jailed on trumped-up charges. And more than a year after his arrest, Leopoldo Lopez, the continent's most high profile political prisoner, continues to languish in prison without a trial, without any semblance of due process. And just last week in an unacceptable and utterly grotesque statement, Venezuelan's Ambassador to the OAS, Roy Chaderton, actually joked about shooting members of the Venezuelan opposition in the head.

Against this backdrop of persecution, violence, and outrageous human rights violations, now even more disturbing trends started to emerge. Just last week, the Treasury Department announced that the Banca Privada d'Andorra, BPA, was involved in a complex scheme to launder nearly $2 billion—let me repeat that—$2 billion in funds from the Venezuelan state oil company, PDVSA. BPA then moved these funds into the U.S. financial system.

In December, a private jet trafficking millions of dollars in cocaine was captured in Fort Lauderdale. In September, a truck carrying $10 million in cash coming from the United States was captured in Venezuela. All of this is on top of the thousands of pounds—literally tons—of cocaine trafficked by the Venezuelan National Guard that has been seized in Europe.

The United States and the international community cannot tolerate such blatant violations of international law. I am pleased that

Treasury has named senior Venezuelan officials as kingpins and acknowledged the Venezuelan National Guard is deeply involved in drug trafficking. Obviously, in today's Venezuela, we are not just watching the rise of an authoritarian regime, we are watching the emergence of a drug trafficking regime involved in networks that threaten and endanger the hemisphere.

So finally, let me just say I welcome the President's decision to move forward with implementation of the Venezuela Defense of Human Rights and Civil Society Act, which, Mr. Chairman, you and I authored and you were deeply involved in helping us draft and ultimately move through the Senate. And I appreciate that—and the announcement last week of targeted sanctions against seven Venezuelan officials, including senior members of the military, intelligence services, and judiciary. In my view, we can go further, but this is an important first step.

Let me reemphasize. These are targeted sanctions against Maduro government officials, not sanctions against the people of Venezuela.

I look forward to hearing the administration's strategy for addressing the political, diplomatic, and security challenges that Venezuela presents.

And I thank you, Mr. Chairman, for the opportunity.

Senator RUBIO. Thank you.

And now we are going to get to our witnesses' testimony.

Just a brief housekeeping item. We will have votes, I think, scheduled at 11 o'clock. There may be a need to go into a brief recess for a few minutes while we go to and from the vote, but we will continue the hearing until we conclude it.

With that, Mr. Lee, we are prepared for your opening statement.

STATEMENT OF ALEX LEE, DEPUTY ASSISTANT SECRETARY FOR SOUTH AMERICA AND CUBA, BUREAU OF WESTERN HEMISPHERE AFFAIRS, U.S. DEPARTMENT OF STATE, WASHINGTON, DC

Mr. LEE. Chairman Rubio, Ranking Member Boxer, and members of the committee, thank you for inviting me to speak to you about Venezuela. I appreciate your interest in Venezuela and your support for United States assistance and our policies there.

We are deeply concerned about the situation in Venezuela where last year legitimate political, economic, and social grievances and a lack of adequate democratic space brought protests and, unfortunately, violence. Tensions within Venezuela continue to build and the government has intensified its actions to repress dissent. The United States has called on the Venezuelan Government to respect human rights, uphold the rule of law, and engage in peaceful, inclusive dialogue with Venezuelans across the political spectrum to alleviate the current tension. We have called on the Venezuelan Government to release Mayor Antonio Ledezma, opposition leader Leopoldo Lopez, Mayor Daniel Ceballos, and others it has unjustly jailed, including dozens of students. We have encouraged the government to improve the climate of respect for human rights and fundamental freedoms, including respect for the freedoms of peaceful assembly and association. I know this committee shares our concerns, and we welcome your strong support for democracy in Venezuela.

Venezuela's problems cannot be solved by criminalizing legitimate democratic dissent. These actions appear to be a clear attempt by the Venezuelan Government to divert attention from that country's economic and political problems. Rather than imprisoning and intimidating its critics, we believe the Venezuelan Government should focus on finding real solutions through democratic dialogue.

We will not refrain from speaking out about human rights abuses in Venezuela. We are joined in this by dozens of individuals and entities, including the U.N. High Commissioner on Human Rights, Organization of American States Secretary General Insulza, the Peruvian, Costa Rican, and Colombian Governments, and the Inter American Commission on Human Rights, among others.

Advancing human rights and democratic processes are a key U.S. foreign policy objective. The President's March 9 Executive order, "Blocking Property and Suspending Entry of Certain Persons Contributing to the Situation in Venezuela," which implements the Venezuela Defense of Human Rights and Civil Society Act of 2014, is a manifestation of our commitment to advancing respect for human rights, safeguarding democratic institutions, and protecting the United States financial system from the illicit financial flows from public corruption in Venezuela.

Executive Order 13692 is aimed at persons involved in, or responsible for, certain conduct in Venezuela, including actions that undermine democratic processes or institutions, the use of violence or conduct that constitutes human rights violations and abuses, including in response to antigovernment protests, actions that prohibit, limit, or penalize the exercise of freedom of expression or peaceful assembly, as well as public corruption by senior government officials in Venezuela. The Executive order does not—repeat—does not target the people or the economy of Venezuela.

I want to be clear. It is not our policy or intent to promote instability in Venezuela or to endorse solutions to Venezuela's problems that are inconsistent with its own legal system. The United States is not seeking the downfall of the Venezuelan Government, nor trying to sabotage the Venezuelan economy. We remain Venezuela's largest trading partner. President Maduro has publicly expressed a desire to improve our bilateral relationship, and we are open to direct communication with the Venezuelan Government. We maintain diplomatic relations and welcome conversations and debate. We remain committed to maintaining our strong and lasting ties with the people of Venezuela. We will not, however, refrain from calling out human rights abuses and other actions and policies that undermine democracy.

We hope the Venezuelan Government will focus its energy on finding real solutions for the country's mounting economic and political problems through democratic dialogue with the political opposition, civil society, and the private sector. This year's National Assembly elections present an opportunity for Venezuelans to engage in legitimate, democratic discourse. And credible election results could reduce tensions in Venezuela. We have urged regional partners to encourage Venezuela to accept a robust international electoral observation mission, using accepted international standards, for those elections. Now is the time for the region to work together to help Venezuela to work toward a democratic solution to the challenges the country faces.

We will also continue to work closely with Congress and others in the region to support greater political expression in Venezuela and to encourage the Venezuelan Government to live up to its required commitments to democracy and human rights, as articulated in the OAS Charter, the Inter American Democratic Charter, and other relevant instruments.

Thank you, and I look forward to answering your questions.

[The prepared statement of Mr. Lee follows:]

PREPARED STATEMENT OF EDWARD ALEXANDER LEE

Chairman Rubio, Ranking Member Boxer, members of the committee, thank you for inviting me to speak with you about Venezuela. I appreciate your interest in Venezuela and your support for U.S. assistance and our policies there.

We are deeply concerned about the situation in Venezuela where last year legitimate political, economic, and social grievances and a lack of adequate democratic space brought protests and, unfortunately, violence. Tensions within Venezuela continue to build and the government has intensified its actions to repress dissent. The United States has called on the Venezuelan Government to respect human rights, uphold the rule of law, and engage in a peaceful, inclusive dialogue with Venezuelans across the political spectrum to alleviate the current tension. We have called on the Venezuelan Government to release Mayor Antonio Ledezma, opposition leader Leopolda Lopez, Mayor Daniel Ceballos, and others it has unjustly jailed, including dozens of students. We have encouraged the government to improve the climate of respect for human rights and fundamental freedoms, including respect for the freedoms of peaceful assembly and association. I know this committee shares our concerns, and we welcome your strong support for democracy in Venezuela.

Venezuela's problems cannot be solved by criminalizing legitimate, democratic dissent. These actions appear to be a clear attempt by the Venezuelan Government to divert attention from that country's economic and political problems. Rather than imprisoning and intimidating its critics, we believe the Venezuelan Government should focus on finding real solutions through democratic dialogue. As I have mentioned, we will not refrain from speaking out about human rights abuses. We are joined in this by dozens of individuals and entities, including the U.N. High Commissioner on Human Rights, Organization of American States (OAS) Secretary General Insulza, the Peruvian, Costa Rican, and Colombian Governments, and the Inter-American Commission on Human Rights, among others.

Advancing human rights and democratic processes are a key U.S. foreign policy objective. The President's March 9 Executive order ''Blocking Property and Suspending Entry of Certain Persons Contributing to the Situation in Venezuela,'' which implements theVenezuela Defense of Human Rights and Civil Society Act of 2014, is a manifestation of our commitment to advancing respect for human rights, safeguarding democratic institutions, and protecting the U.S. fmancial system from the illicit financial flows from public coruption in Venezuela.

Executive Order 13692 is aimed at persons involved in, or responsible for, certain conduct in Venezuela, including actions that undermine democratic processes or institutions, the use of violence or conduct that constitutes human rights violations and abuses, including in response to antigovernment protests, actions that prohibit, limit, or penalize the exercise of freedom of expression or peaceful assembly, as well as public corruption by senior government officials in Venezuela. The Executive order does not target the people or the economy of Venezuela.

I want to be clear: it is not our policy or intent to promote instability in Venezuela or to endorse solutions to Venezuela's political problems that are inconsistent with its own legal system. The United States is not seeking the downfall of the Venezuelan Government nor trying to sabotage the Venezuelan economy. We remain Venezuela's largest trading partner. President Maduro publicly expresses a desire to improve our bilateral relationship, and we are open to direct communication with the Venezuelan Government. We maintain diplomatic relations and welcome conversations and debate. We remain committed to maintaining our strong and lasting ties with the people of Venezuela. We will not, however, refrain from calling out human rights abuses and other actions and policies that undermine democracy.

We hope the Venezuelan Government will focus its energy on finding real solutions for the country's mounting economic and political problems through democratic dialogue with the political opposition, civil society, and the private sector. This year's National Assembly elections present an opportunity for Venezuelans to engage in legitimate, democratic discourse. And, credible election results could reduce tensions in Venezuela. We have urged regional partners to encourage Venezuela to accept a robust international electoral observation mission, using accepted international standards, for those elections. Now is the time for the region to work together to help Venezuela to work toward a democratic solution to the challenges the country faces.

We will also continue to work closely with Congress and others in the region to support greater political expression in Venezuela, and to encourage the Venezuelan Government to live up to its required commitments to democracy and human rights, as articulated in the OAS Charter, the Inter-American Democratic Charter, and other relevant instruments.

Mr. Chairman, I would like to end by saying that we sincerely appreciate the Senate Foreign Relations Committee's contributions to the promotion of human rights in Venezuela. The strong, bipartisan cooperation among this committee's members and staff to support the State Department's championing of democracy, human rights, and freedom of expression throughout the hemisphere is a credit to our great country.

Senator RUBIO. Thank you.
Mr. Smith.

STATEMENT OF JOHN SMITH, ACTING DIRECTOR OF THE OFFICE OF FOREIGN ASSETS CONTROL, U.S. DEPARTMENT OF THE TREASURY, WASHINGTON, DC

Mr. SMITH. Chairman Rubio, Ranking Member Boxer, distinguished members of the committee, thank you for the invitation to appear before you today at this important hearing on political and economic developments in Venezuela, the human rights situation in the country, and the implications of these topics for regional stability and United States interests. I will address the administration's implementation of the sanctions measures in the Venezuela Defense of Human Rights and Civil Society Act of 2014, which was signed into law in December.

On March 9, the President issued an Executive order declaring a national emergency with respect to the situation in Venezuela, which is a prerequisite for the imposition of economic sanctions under the International Emergency Economic Powers Act. The Executive order, which implements the targeted economic sanctions contained in the act and builds on them in key respects, imposes economic sanctions on persons listed in an annex to the order and any persons determined by the Secretary of the Treasury, in consultation with the Secretary of State, to have engaged in, or to have been responsible for, certain enumerated activities in relation to Venezuela such as undermining democratic processes or institutions, committing serious abuses or violations of human rights, limiting or penalizing the exercise of freedom of expression or peaceful assembly, or being involved in public corruption by senior Venezuelan Government officials.

The Executive order also contains a status-based authority targeting current and former officials of the Government of Venezuela, which gives the Secretary of the Treasury additional flexibility to go after targets of concern for which there may be limitations on our ability to designate under the other conduct-based authorities.

The President named seven Venezuelan individuals in the annex to the order. The property and interests in property of these individuals are blocked, meaning their assets within U.S. jurisdiction are frozen, and U.S. persons are prohibited from engaging in any transactions or dealings with them.

Last week's action imposing sanctions on seven individuals focused on those involved in human rights abuses and the persecution of political opponents connected to the events surrounding the February 2014 protests highlighted in the act. Most of the individuals targeted are currently, or were formerly associated with, Venezuela's National Guard, the Armed Forces, the intelligence service, or the national police, members of which played key roles in repression against individuals involved in the protests. The Executive order also targeted a national-level prosecutor who was charged, based in part on implausible and/or fabricated information, several opposition members with conspiring to assassinate or overthrow President Maduro.

Mr. Chairman, I want to acknowledge the leadership you have demonstrated on this issue, and I note that six of the seven targets in the annex to the Executive order were included in your list of individuals published last May.

In addition to implementing the act, the order expands the designation criteria beyond the requirements of the act. This will allow greater targeting flexibility and the highlighting, targeting, and deterrence of additional problematic behavior that is ongoing in Venezuela. We remain committed to defending human rights, advancing democratic governance, and protecting the U.S. financial system from abuse.

To be clear and as the chairman and ranking member and fellow speakers have said, these sanctions are not aimed against the country of Venezuela. They do not target the Venezuelan people, nor do they sanction the Venezuelan Government as a whole. To the contrary, this remains a targeted sanctions program focused tightly and precisely on bad actors undermining Venezuela's democracy, violating the human rights of its citizens, and diverting much-needed economic resources for personal gain, resources that could and should be invested for the public good.

Turning specifically to the sanctions program's focus on public corruption in Venezuela, I would echo President Obama, who has said that fighting corruption is one of the great struggles of our time. Corruption, beyond its unethical nature, siphons off important resources that could be used to feed children or build schools and infrastructure that promote development.

It is also worth noting the long history of the application of United States sanctions to foreign policy and national security concerns with a Venezuelan nexus. Even before this past year's events, we have not hesitated to designate Venezuelan banks and other companies for their connections with Iranian entities sanctioned for nuclear proliferation activities, as well as designating Venezuelan targets for their links to narcotics trafficking.

As I conclude these remarks, I want to emphasize that we retain the ability to respond to events in Venezuela as they unfold. We stand ready with a powerful financial tool to deter abuses and target those who may choose to undermine democratic processes or institutions or to violate human rights in Venezuela.

Thank you.

[The prepared statement of Mr. Smith follows:]

PREPARED STATEMENT OF JOHN E. SMITH

VENEZUELA SANCTIONS PROGRAM

Chairman Rubio, Ranking Member Boxer, distinguished members of the committee, thank you for the invitation to appear before you today at this important hearing on political and economic developments in Venezuela, the human rights situation in the country, and the implications of these topics for regional stability and U.S. interests. As the Acting Director of the Treasury Department's Office of Foreign Assets Control (OFAC), I will address the administration's implementation of the sanctions measures in the Venezuela Defense of Human Rights and Civil Society Act of 2014 (the Act), which was signed into law on December 18, 2014.

Executive Order 13692

On March 9, the President issued Executive Order 13692 declaring a national emergency with respect to the situation in Venezuela, which is a prerequisite for the imposition of economic sanctions under the International Emergency Economic Powers Act (IEEPA). The Executive order, which implements the targeted sanctions contained in the Act and builds on them in key respects, imposes economic sanctions on persons listed in an Annex to the Order and any persons determined by the Secretary of the Treasury, in consultation with the Secretary of State, to have engaged in, or to have been responsible for, certain enumerated activities in relation to Venezuela such as undermining democratic processes or institutions, committing serious abuses or violations of human rights, limiting or penalizing the exercise of freedom of expression or peaceful assembly, or being involved in public corruption by senior Venezuelan Government officials. The Executive order also contains a "status-based" authority targeting current and former officials of the Government of Venezuela, which gives the Secretary of the Treasury additional flexibility to go after targets of concern for which there may be limitations on our ability to designate under the other "conduct-based" authorities. The President named seven Venezuelan individuals in the Annex to the Order. The property and interests in property of these individuals are blocked, meaning their assets within U.S. jurisdiction are frozen, and U.S. persons are prohibited from engaging in any transactions or dealings with them. The Executive order also suspends the entry into the United States of individuals who are determined to meet the criteria for economic sanctions.

Last week's action imposing sanctions on seven individuals focused on those involved in human rights abuses and the persecution of political opponents connected to the events surrounding the February 2014 protests highlighted in the Act. Most of the individuals targeted are currently or were formerly associated with Venezuela's National Guard, the Armed Forces, the intelligence service, or the national police, members of which played key roles in repression against individuals involved in the protests beginning in February 2014. The Executive order also targeted a national-level prosecutor who has charged—based in part on implausible and/or fabricated information—several opposition members with conspiring to assassinate or overthrow President Maduro. Mr. Chairman, I want to acknowledge the leadership you have demonstrated on this issue, and I would note that six of the seven targets in the Annex to the Executive order were included in your list of individuals published in May of last year.

In addition to implementing the Act, the order expands the designation criteria beyond the requirements of the Act. This will allow for greater targeting flexibility and the highlighting, targeting, and deterrence of additional problematic behavior that is ongoing in Venezuela. We remain committed to defending human rights, advancing democratic governance in Venezuela, and protecting the U.S. financial system from abuse.

Building on the Legislation

While the Act focuses on human rights abuses specifically related to last year's protests, the Executive order expands our targeting authority to more broadly cover any significant acts of violence or serious violations of human rights in relation to Venezuela, and restrictions on the exercise of freedom of expression or peaceful assembly in Venezuela, allowing us to deter and address repression as it may arise. The order also includes designation criteria related to the undermining of democracy in Venezuela and to public corruption by senior Venezuelan Government officials.

Finally, the E.O. gives us the discretionary authority to designate current or former Venezuelan Government officials. As we have learned from experience across a number of sanctions programs, this type of "status-based" authority is a useful tool that allows us to go after targets of concern for which there may be limitations to our ability to designate under "conduct-based" authorities.

To be clear, these sanctions are not aimed against the country of Venezuela. They do not target the Venezuelan people or the economy, nor do they sanction the Venezuelan Government as a whole. To the contrary, this remains a targeted sanctions program focused tightly and precisely on bad actors undermining Venezuela's democracy, violating and abusing the human rights of its citizens, and diverting much-needed economic resources for personal gain—resources that could and should be invested for the public good.

Public Corruption

Turning specifically to this sanctions program's focus on public corruption in Venezuela, I would echo President Obama, who has said that fighting corruption is one of the great struggles of our time. Corruption, beyond its unethical nature, siphons off important resources that could be used to feed children or build schools and infrastructure that promote development.

As the largest economy in the world, we remain Venezuela's primary trading partner and maintain financial ties to Venezuela. These relationships, while a natural outcome of our long-standing economic engagement with the region, also potentially expose our financial system to illicit financial flows from public corruption in Venezuela, as Venezuelan Government officials who control access to scarce U.S. dollars attempt to take advantage to reap illicit gains. This close interaction with the U.S. financial system, however, also gives us leverage from a sanctions perspective. Venezuela's heavy use of the U.S. dollar and Venezuelans' frequent travel to the United States make targets of our sanctions vulnerable. We expect our designations will have bite.

In addition, Treasury is using the full range of its financial tools to address the exploitation of the U.S. financial system in furtherance of corruption schemes. Last week, for example, the Financial Crimes Enforcement Network (FinCEN) of the Department of the Treasury issued a public notice of finding that Banca Privada d'Andorra (BPA) is a financial institution operating outside of the United States that is of a "primary money laundering concern." The finding that accompanied this notice outlined how a third-party money launderer in Venezuela worked with BPA to deposit the proceeds of public corruption, some of which transited the U.S. financial system, into an account at BPA. This network was well connected to Venezuelan Government officials and facilitated the movement of at least $50 million through the United States from 2011 to 2013 in support of this money laundering network.

Narcotics, Terrorism, and Iran

It is also worth noting the long history of the application of U.S. sanctions to foreign policy and national security concerns with a Venezuela nexus. Even before the past year's events, we have not hesitated to designate Venezuelan banks and other companies for their connections with Iranian entities sanctioned for nuclear proliferation activities pursuant to our counterproliferation authorities. These actions included the designation of the International Development Bank in Caracas, a subsidiary of the Tehran-based Export Development Bank of Iran.

Our actions to combat narcotics trafficking in Latin America pursuant to the Foreign Narcotics Kingpin Designation Act have proceeded to a steady drumbeat, and they have not overlooked Venezuelan targets. For example, in September 2011, OFAC designated four Venezuelan Government officials for acting for, or on behalf of, the FARC, a designated narcoterrorist organization. The four officials acted in direct support of the FARC's narcotics and arms trafficking activities in Venezuela. In September 2012, shortly after his arrest in Panama, OFAC designated a Venezuelan narcotics trafficker and his company. The trafficker was previously indicted in the Southern District of Florida on cocaine trafficking charges. And in August 2013, OFAC designated a former Venezuelan National Guard captain as a significant foreign narcotics trafficker. The captain had previously been indicted in the Eastern District of New York in March 2011 on multiple cocaine trafficking charges. He facilitated cocaine loads from Colombia through Venezuela in partnership with well-known narcotics traffickers in Colombia and Mexico.

We have also acted to constrain Lebanese Hezbollah activity in Venezuela, designating in 2008 Hezbollah supporters and fundraisers active in Venezuela pursuant to our counterterrorism sanctions authorities. One of the targets was a senior Venezuelan diplomat who had facilitated the travel of Hezbollah members to and from Venezuela.

CONCLUSION

Before I conclude these remarks, I want to emphasize that we retain the ability to respond to events in Venezuela as they unfold. We stand ready with a powerful financial tool to deter abuses and target those who may choose to undermine democratic processes or institutions. In concert with this Congress, we have made clear that the United States will not stand idly by and witness the repression that has occurred in Venezuela this past year. We have demonstrated in numerous and diverse scenarios across the globe that the United States has the ability to target those involved in human rights abuses and the undermining of democracy and to prevent them from accessing the United States financial system. And when we do so, they will find themselves isolated domestically, regionally, and globally.

Senator RUBIO. Thank you both for being here and for your opening testimony.

I will begin the questioning round. We will do 7 minutes since I think we will have time to get through all of this.

Let me begin with you, Mr. Lee. I wanted to talk to you about the political state in Venezuela. So as I have outlined in my opening statements and so has the ranking member and the ranking member of the full committee, in Venezuela there is an increased encroachment on freedom of the press and communication. There has been an increased encroachment on the judiciary branch. It no longer truly operates as an independent branch. We have seen the prosecutorial powers used to not just fabricate evidence but to target political opponents. We have seen members of the opposition expelled by simple majority votes from the National Assembly. We have seen the jailing of virtually every prominent—at some point, virtually every prominent voice in Venezuela that opposes the Maduro government. And there is now this pattern of decree powers that have been given to Maduro, including the one this weekend.

Is Venezuela still a democracy?

Mr. LEE. The Venezuelan electoral system is actually quite good in terms of the mechanical process. What the government has done is used a variety of means, gerrymandering, massive use of public funds, trumped-up charges against key opposition people, a systematic undermining of the independence of the media to tilt all the electoral ground in its favor. That still does not change the reality of how Venezuelans view the situation in Venezuela or how they perceive the government's handling. And if you look at polling, the polling shows that the majority of Venezuelans view the government mismanaging the economy and things are getting worse.

We call on the Venezuelan Government to announce elections. We call on the Venezuelan Government to hold those elections in a way that provides the political space for the opposition, and we believe that if that is done and, in particular, if the international community can provide electoral monitoring of those elections, the Venezuelan people will have an opportunity to express their views.

Senator RUBIO. Well, thank you, Mr. Lee. And I appreciate your answer, and I understand it. I would just suggest that we need to view this from a different perspective because in Latin America, there is a troubling trend, and that is, people come to power through an election and then begin to undermine all the apparatus of a free society. So if I am a member of the opposition and there is no free press that can cover my activities, because they are not allowed to operate, so I have no way to get my word out, Maduro has unfettered access to the national airwaves, I have no access to the national airwaves. If I speak out too vehemently against him in the National Assembly, I could be removed and arrested. First they remove you so they can strip you of the immunity of being a deputy, and then they arrest you for it. And not to mention that there is evidence of electoral fraud in the last elections.

You combine all these things—and just because you have an election, or say you had an election, does not make it a free and fair election. This is the pattern that has been followed in places like Nicaragua and other places as well. There is more to democracy than just holding an election. And certainly they are capable of having a free and fair election mechanically, but when the people running against you cannot go on the airwaves, cannot have TV shows, cannot speak out or they will be arrested, the entire media is owned by your cronies, you have unfettered access to the airwaves, they have none, and if you are part of the opposition and you oppose Maduro, you can be arrested, in my mind that does not sound like a democratic society.

And I think it is important for us to understand that this is the new way tyrants are now operating. They dress themselves up as democrat, but then they end up governing in much different ways. And that is an important distinction for us to point to.

I want to get to the issue of individuals. There are a number of individuals that were not sanctioned that I would encourage us to continue to look at. For example, last year Generals Aref Jimenez and Julio Cesar Morales Prieto, who held senior positions in Venezuela's directorate of armaments and explosives, played a key role in their efforts to create and support the government-affiliated colectivos. There was basically already regular armed groups. The DAEX, by the way, is currently led by Gen. Ignacio Velasquez Ramos. This is a group that has been intricately involved in cracking down on dissent.

Of the seven designated individuals that constitute a national security threat to the United States, their bosses are not represented. For example, Gen. Vladimir Padrino, the Minister of Defense and as such, the highest ranking military officer, has not been held responsible for human rights violations committed by his subordinates. Some of the sanctions were based on Venezuelan officials allegedly involved in corruption and illicit activities, but we did not include Diosdado Cabello, the head of the Parliament who has been identified by defectors and others as the head of the cartel, the Los Solis, a drug cartel operated by Venezuelan generals.

And then there is multiple print and broadcast reports, articles, and even books detailing the presence in the United States of Chavez and Maduro government officials that have become fabulously wealthy from what are alleged to be corrupt activities. They too use our financial system to transfer funds. One example is an individual by the name of Alejandro Andrade, who is a former army lieutenant and a fellow plotter of Chavez in the 1992 attempted coup that cost the lives of over 300 Venezuelans and who was later appointed by Chavez as the treasurer of the country. He is reported to be living in multimillion dollar equestrian estate in south Florida. And there are many other former officials, bankers, and business executives also living or owning property in the United States that are alleged to have acquired fortunes illicitly with the complicity of the Chavez/Maduro government. And I would encourage you to look at some of them as well.

Mr. Smith, has the Treasury looked at certain financial institutions in Venezuela or the Venezuelan banking system as a whole to see who might qualify as financial institutions of primary money laundering concern under section 311 of the USA PATRIOT Act?

Mr. SMITH. Senator, I can tell you that with respect to many of the names that you talked about, we continue to investigate vigorously under all of the prongs of the Executive order. Unfortunately, you are asking me about authority, the particular one with respect to the financial institution—you are asking me about an authority that is administered by one of my sister agencies, the Financial Crimes Enforcement Network, and I can take that question back to them.

Senator RUBIO. Well, let me just encourage you to act on information my office has received and to money laundering carried out by the petroleum company, PDVSA—P-D-V-S-A. There are close ties, according to these allegations and information that I have received between this organization and money laundering and drug trafficking activity. And there are a number of names that have been forwarded to us as individuals involved in this illicit activity: Rafael Ramirez, Nervis Gerardo Villalobos, Omar Farias, Carlos Luis, Aguilera Borjas, Alcides Rondon, and Rafael Jimenez Villaroel. We have received significant information about their ties between the state-run oil entity and drug trafficking and other laundering activities within Venezuela. And I will have more on this topic in a moment, but I want to recognize the ranking member.

Senator BOXER. Thanks so much, Mr. Chairman.

Gentlemen, whoever feels comfortable answering these questions. President Obama's Executive order imposing sanctions on Venezuelan officials implicated in human rights violations and corruption was met with widespread criticism from Latin American nations. This is very upsetting to a lot of us. At a special meeting in Ecuador on Saturday, the 12-nation Union of South American Nations issued a statement criticizing the U.S. action as ''an interventionist threat to sovereignty and the principle of noninterference in the internal affairs of other countries,'' and calling for the Executive order to be rescinded.

In addition, President Maduro has said he will use next month's Summit of the Americas in Panama to denounce the sanctions.

What steps are we taking to engage with Latin American nations about the recently announced sanctions? Have any countries in the region expressed support for our action?

Mr. LEE. I will start and then my colleague will finish, Senator.

Senator BOXER. Okay.

Mr. LEE. We need to balance our condemnation of the human rights violations, which came through loud and clear with the law and the Executive order, as well as the various U.S. Government statements over the past 2 years, with the need to convince the region to act——

Senator BOXER. Wait a minute. Just tell me. Are there any nations who support what we did in Latin America, and what are we doing to make sure they understand that what we did was the right thing, the moral thing, the correct thing for the people of Venezuela? So instead of reading me something, I know it is diplomacy and I understand all that. But on the ground, are we talking with our friends in region? Because it is upsetting to me that we see so little support.

Mr. LEE. Senator, you are right that the Latin American community has sharply criticized our sanctions against individual Venezuelans. We have made a full court press to explain that what we are doing represents our principles and that we are exercising our own sovereignty in not allowing human rights violators or corrupt actors to come into our country or to enjoy our financial system.

At the same time, we point out that and we urge the other Latin American countries to provide greater efforts with the Venezuelan Government to try to bridge the differences within Venezuela——

Senator BOXER. Okay. So just to cut through. We are working with our friends in the region to get them to understand why what we did was right. Yes or no?

Mr. LEE. Yes.

Senator BOXER. Okay. And will the crisis in Venezuela be a priority for President Obama when he attends the Summit of the Americas?

Mr. LEE. Yes, ma'am.

Senator BOXER. And how do United States sanctions fit into a broader United States strategy to address the growing crisis in Venezuela? In other words, what else are we doing besides the sanctions, besides talking to other nations? Do we have anything else that we are working on?

Mr. LEE. The greatest chance for Venezuela to solve its problems is holding a credible electoral process, and for that, we need to work with the international community, particularly Venezuela's neighbors. And we were encouraged that UNASUR recently, after its meeting in Quito, issued for the first time a statement that has called on Venezuelans to engage in dialogue and to hold an election to try to bridge the differences, and we believe that is a positive step forward. We would like our Latin American partners to more vigorously champion the need for an electoral monitoring mission in Venezuela. But, yes, we are constantly engaged with likeminded countries, and we have seen a growing appreciation in Latin America that the economic situation in Venezuela is untenable and the Venezuelan Government's effort to try to control political opposition to it through repression is only greatly exacerbating the problem.

Senator BOXER. Well, I want to say thank you for that. I agree with you that this upcoming election is critical. It is absolutely critical. And I agree with the comments made by my chairman here about having a vote and then having someone elected and declaring martial law and taking over and saying I can just decree this, that, and the other. That is what is going on.

But later this year, Venezuela is expected to hold their parliamentary elections, and opposition leaders view these elections as an important chance to gain seats in the National Assembly and enable the opposition to put pressure on Maduro, particularly as his approval ratings have plummeted. So your point of focusing on the election—I really appreciate that, and I think that is what we should all focus on because I think clearly, if you look at what the people are saying in terms of their suffering and the rest, this could be a very important turning point—this election—if it is free and fair.

And I am concerned about the lack of support in the region for our sanctions, and I think we should tell, as you are already, our friends in the region that it is our right as a nation not to allow people to come here and hide their money and all the rest of it. That is our right as a sovereign nation. And if we can build support, pivot to this upcoming election, I think it is absolutely crucial. And if it is not free and fair and if there is suppression, it is very dangerous.

So I want to again thank my chairman for these very important hearings and thank both of you for your contribution.

Senator RUBIO. Thank you, Senator Boxer.

Senator Gardner.

Senator GARDNER. Thank you all to the witnesses for being here today, and I join Chairman Rubio and other members of the subcommittee in expressing my utmost concern about the state of affairs in Venezuela.

Given his dwindling public support, it seems that President Maduro has inherited all the authoritarian instincts of the late Hugo Chavez but none of his charm.

I commend the administration for imposing additional sanctions on Venezuelan officials last week, though that action has predictively ushered in hysterical reaction from Caracas. I look forward to working with the committee to ensure that genuine democracy returns to Venezuela in our lifetime.

We have had a lot of conversations this morning about the elections and the order. And so given the United States sanctions announcement, the Venezuelan National Assembly has granted President Maduro the power to govern by decree until the end of 2015. Mr. Lee, you talked about the mechanical process of elections being good or sound in Venezuela, at least at this point. Do you see, leading up to the elections, this decree power, and what should we look for? Do you see it impacting the election, and what should we look for in terms of their ability to tilt the playing field, as you mentioned some of the things they have been trying to do in the past?

Mr. LEE. Well, we are clearly concerned that President Maduro might use his decree powers in a way that would complicate even more the ability to hold free and fair elections. We will have to see how he uses his decree powers, which last until the end of the year, or during the period in which the elections are going to be held.

Again, I think that one of the most effective ways to pressure the Venezuelan Government to do the right thing with regard to elections is to encourage the international community, and in particular Venezuela's Latin American neighbors, to emphasize to the government the absolute importance of holding free and fair elections. Democracy and the commitment to support democracy is not only an obligation by Venezuela under the OAS but in many of its other subregional organizations that it is a member of, including MERCOSUR and UNASUR. And so we very much want the other countries in the region to try to help broker an understanding between the government and the opposition to provide the conditions for an election that is viewed as credible by all. We believe that is as a solution would go a long, long way to addressing some of the major, major problems that the country is facing.

Senator GARDNER. Thank you, Mr. Lee.

Mr. Smith, kind of following up on those comments, what has the reaction been to our sanctions in the region, and have we coordinated these sanctions with any of our allies in the region such as Brazil or Colombia?

Mr. SMITH. I will defer to my State Department colleague to talk about the reaction in the region. I will say that we do coordinate with allies in the region and allies around the world as we can. And so most of the time, we have what is called a prenotification process where we work with other countries to give them notification of what we are going to do so they may not be surprised and they can work with us.

Senator GARDNER. Thank you.

Mr. Lee, do the anti-U.S. demonstrations on the streets of Caracas and elsewhere represent a security threat to remaining U.S. diplomatic and civilian personnel or their interests?

Mr. LEE. Clearly, you know, the safety of our staff in Caracas is paramount just like the safety of American citizens living in Venezuela is paramount. Up to now, we have not seen targeting of Americans per se. So for that, we are encouraged.

Senator GARDNER. Have we taken any precautions? Has the State Department taken any precautions to protect our citizens and diplomats?

Mr. LEE. Yes, sir. We have a system to notify Americans residing in Venezuela whenever we are aware of information suggesting that Americans may be targeted or there may be disturbances. And so we have a network that we use to get that information out.

Our Embassy also is constantly reviewing its posture with respect to any possible disturbances. And so this is something that we just do as a matter of course.

Senator GARDNER. Mr. Chairman, I know we have votes coming up. So I will yield back my time so that you can get some other questions.

Senator RUBIO. Thank you.

Senator Menendez.

Senator MENENDEZ. Thank you, Mr. Chairman.

Mr. Lee, I listened to your statement, and I have to wonder. I do not know why one would even suggest or have to feel the necessity to say that we are not trying to promote instability in Venezuela. We clearly are not trying to promote instability in Venezuela. But if we are going to make that statement about human rights and democracy anyplace in the world—forget about Venezuela—we are in a sad state of affairs. This is not an American view. This is what the OAS Charter says. This is what the Inter-American Democratic Charter says. This is what the U.N. Declaration of Human Rights entails.

So when you say that and then when you say—and I cannot believe that you included it in your opening remarks, suggesting that President Maduro wants to improve our bilateral relationships. Yes, that is a good way to do it by unilaterally striking at reducing our Embassy and taking a whole host of other aggressive and active postures against the United States. It boggles my imagination.

It also worries me when the State Department in a different context—I know you were down in Cuba before all the announcements. I guess I should have seen your effusiveness as a sign of things to come. And then see that others in the Department talked about it is not who you invite to the table, speaking to the Summit of the Americas, but what you speak about. Well, here we are with both Cuba, which of course has no democracy and human rights, and Venezuela, under which democracy and human rights are a deep threat. And I do not get the sense that the State Department has the drive and the conviction of these views by actions.

I think it would be fair to say that we allowed the Latin Americans, when Senator Rubio and I were pursuing the legislation, which we thought was necessary to do—we were asked by the administration and told by the administration we are trying to allow our Latin American partners to get Maduro to move in a different direction. Is that not fair to say that we did try? We gave them space and time to try to achieve that.

Mr. LEE. Yes, you did.

Senator MENENDEZ. And they did not succeed.

Now, I look at the President's own declaration, which I applaud, and I look at drug trafficking—where do drugs end up? They end up on the streets of our cities. They end up addicting our young people. That is a national security threat. That would be whether it is Venezuela or any other part of the world. When you look at the amount of drug trafficking by Venezuela, when you look at the specifics of our own administration, the naming the Venezuelan National Guard as part of this process, I just do not quite get it as it relates to the statements that are made by the Department. The Venezuelan National Guard, members of the military directly involved in narcotics trafficking.

Mr. Smith, we have this $2 billion—this comes after—$2 billion. Even here, that is not chump change. Two billion dollars that ultimately works its way into the United States financial system; $2 billion taken from the people of Venezuela because PDVSA is, in essence, the national patrimony of Venezuela. And I think the people of Venezuela, who are suffering enormously as a result of the Maduro government, would be far better off with having those $2 billion in Venezuela helping their lives. So how are we acting as it relates to these $2 billion that made its way into the United States financial system?

Mr. SMITH. So, sir, I can say the Treasury Department has been engaged in vigorous actions across the board, and for many of the activities that you have been talking about, we have been working for years on narcotics trafficking. We have designated across the board narcotics traffickers——

Senator MENENDEZ. I appreciate it. Talk to me about the $2 billion.

Mr. SMITH. When you asked about the $2 billion, that was an action that one of my sister agencies, the Financial Crimes Enforcement Network, took, and that is the agency that I would have to refer this question back to.

Senator MENENDEZ. Okay. So you have nothing to do with that.

Mr. SMITH. It is another part of my Department.

Senator MENENDEZ. So you cannot speak to that.

Can you speak to that, Mr. Lee?

Mr. LEE. No, sir.

Senator MENENDEZ. Oh, my God. We come to a hearing on Venezuela. There are $2 billion siphoned out of PDVSA, and no one is capable of responding to it. It is amazing. It is amazing.

Let me ask you this. The actions that have been taken under our legislation—while I recognize the convenience of responding to Venezuelan sanctions against seven U.S. officials with parity, the parameters set forth in our legislation and their expansion under the President's Executive order leaves many other Venezuelan officials eligible given their complicity in human rights abuses, certainly more than the seven that have been named. I and other members have specifically called for Defense Minister Vladimir Padrino Lopez to be added to the list of sanctioned individuals given his role in authorizing the use of lethal force against unarmed citizens.

To that end, do you agree that current United States law clearly leaves other Venezuelan officials eligible to be targeted for sanctions?

Mr. LEE. Clearly we have, as a result of the law and the Executive order, the authorities to use against human rights violators and senior officials engaged in corrupt action.

Senator MENENDEZ. It is a simple question. I am not asking you who. I am asking you do you believe that the law allows you to pursue other Venezuelan authorities who may, in fact, fall in the categories as determined both by the law and the President's Executive order.

Mr. LEE. Yes.

Senator MENENDEZ. Or, Mr. Smith, if you are the appropriate person——

Mr. SMITH. Yes, sir.

Senator MENENDEZ. Yes. Okay.

And finally, can you tell me what we are doing about how OFAC makes a kingpin designation? What are the implications and consequences in pursuing kingpin designations, which several people here have been in Venezuela?

Mr. SMITH. Sure. OFAC works with a broad interagency group that is specified in the statute to make kingpin designations. We gather the evidence. We compile it. We run it through to make sure that there are no law enforcement or intelligence equities, and then we make the kingpin designations. The President has the authority to make what are called the Tier 1 designations of significant foreign trafficking individuals or entities, and then OFAC has the authority to make those that are Tier 2, the material support and others. Last year we did over 200 kingpin designations. It is one of our most active programs, and we continue to pursue those vigorously.

Senator MENENDEZ. Thank you, Mr. Chairman.

Senator RUBIO. Thank you.

Senator Perdue.

Senator PERDUE. Thank you, Mr. Chairman. I will be very brief. We have a vote coming up, and I would ask the panel to be brief. I just have a couple questions.

First of all, the United States is enabling a dictatorial regime in Venezuela in my mind as it continues to routinely violate human rights affairs there in Venezuela, I would argue primarily because we continue to rely on imports of oil produced in their state-run enterprises. It seems somewhat hypocritical to me to want to limit what others are doing in Venezuela while we are quite happy to continue to import $30 billion of oil each year. It is another reason why projects like Keystone continue to be critical to reduce our dependence on oil from bad actors like Venezuela.

But I want to go to a separate issue and that is Cuba. You know, last year Venezuelan President Maduro referred to President Obama's shift in policy toward Cuba as ''a gesture of courage.'' Will this opening of United States relations with Cuba hurt or help our situation in trying to change behavior with Maduro? And what impact will this change in Cuba policy have on our long-term effort here to bring democracy back to Venezuela?

Mr. LEE. Well, Senator, diplomacy is not a one-size-fit-all. And so we basically have to kind of see where the opportunities are, make our decisions on what will best advance our national interests. And we have decided, for example, that it advances our national interests to combine, with regard to Venezuela, sanctions and reaching out to other Latin American likeminded countries to urge the Venezuelan Government to meet its democratic obligations. And so that is one strategy that we have used toward——

Senator PERDUE. I am sorry. Let me get to the point. We are going to run out of time and we are going to have to bolt.

Specifically, if we move to a more liberal relationship with Cuba, what specific impact will that have on Maduro in his continuing dominance of his people in Venezuela?

Mr. LEE. I am not sure that there will be a direct relationship.

Senator PERDUE. Okay. Thank you.

The next is, you know, given the difficult situation in Venezuela—they have an oil economy basically. And as I see it down there, the consumer is really not able to bring their economy back. But how is this going to hurt their financing program, Petrocaribe, or its extensive support to Cuba?

Mr. LEE. I think Venezuela's mounting economic problems manifest itself in a whole variety of ways, but one of them clearly is an inability to sustain the support to Petrocaribe like it had in the past. We have seen reports of Venezuela cutting back its subsidized support through Petrocaribe to a variety of Caribbean countries, and so that really puts into question the ability of Venezuela to maintain the level of support it had promised in the past.

Senator PERDUE. So one last quick question. If we really want to change behavior in Venezuela, oil is the way to do it. I just do not believe these sanctions go far enough to really change behavior. We see it in other parts of the world, Russia particularly. When we started out with similar sanctions there, it had no impact.

Mr. Smith, what do you believe would be the impact if we really were to get serious about changing behavior in Venezuela to go after the oil? And that means that we would have to pay a price, too, because the oil that we bring in, the $30 billion, is done in JV's I think with U.S. corporations with their state-owned oil enterprise.

Mr. LEE. May I answer?

Senator PERDUE. Yes, please.

Mr. LEE. After consulting with a variety of civil society actors and political actors in Venezuela, we have made the decision that it really advances United States interests not to use sectoral sanctions in Venezuela.

Senator PERDUE. What is that? I am sorry.

Mr. LEE. To use like an oil sanction.

Senator PERDUE. So specifically, we think that these sanctions will change the behavior of this despot in Venezuela.

Mr. LEE. We believe the sanctions, under the authorities that we have as a result, help highlight unacceptable behavior——

Senator PERDUE. How long do you think it will take to change that behavior specifically?

Mr. LEE. I cannot say.

Senator PERDUE. Well, what is a reasonable person's estimate?

Mr. LEE. I really cannot say.

Senator PERDUE. Let me ask it differently. So how long would we be patient to watch the human rights violations in Venezuela before we stiffen those sanctions?

Mr. LEE. We think that if Venezuela is going to stop this downward slide, it is basically through more democracy and the best way to express that is through holding elections that are seen as credible. And we believe that the international community can play a role toward that. I think we need to combine the use of sanctions against individuals in order to express our democratic principles——

Senator PERDUE. I am sorry to interrupt. But those sanctions against individuals—we have really very little evidence around the world that sanctions against individuals have ever really changed behavior. So, again, I think it is more a question now let us see how long it is going to take. My question is, What is a reasonable expectation on our part of these sanctions relative to changing behavior? It is one thing to have an election, as we just talked about, but to have a credible election to give a free vote for the people down there—I mean, what should be a reasonable timeframe while we wait for these to take effect?

Mr. LEE. I cannot say, sir.

Senator PERDUE. Thank you very much.

Senator RUBIO. Thank you.

I am going to wait for Senator Kaine to return because we are in the middle of this vote, and I appreciate your questions.

So let me, Mr. Lee, just touch on the issue of human rights. They have been well documented, we know, some of them that have already happened. I want to inform you of a couple more that I hope the State Department will look at closely as we continue to examine other people that can be sanctioned.

The first is—have you been made aware of a facility that is colloquially referred to as La Tumba, The Tomb? Have you heard that term?

Mr. LEE. No, sir.

Senator RUBIO. Okay. Well, let me tell you about it based on the information we have received. It is a detention area that is located four stories below the Plaza Venezuela, which is a SEBIN station where detainees are held captive in 2-to-3-meter-sized rooms. They are subjected to minimum temperatures and permanent neon lighting and denied sunlight so that they can become disoriented and suffer physical and psychological deterioration. We have also received information that Gabriel Valles, Gerardo Caredo, and Lorent Saleh have been held captive in that facility and are subjected to this torture. The purpose of this treatment is to coerce from them false testimony against members of the opposition.

I also want to make you aware of the circumstances surrounding the death of Rodolfo Gonzalez. The information we have received—obviously, he was an opposition activist, a senior citizen, and he was jailed in a SEBIN facility beginning in April 2014, supposedly for conspiring against the government, which was actually false. During this time, he was visited by Iris Varela, who is the minister of the national prison system days before his apparent suicide while in custody.

And according to the information we have received, Varela threatened to transfer him to a general population prison, basically with other common criminals—with common criminals—not other common criminals. He was instructed to gather his personal belongings and he was even taken to a prison medic for an examination prior to this transfer.

According to the information provided to us, Mr. Gonzalez's lawyer has confirmed that he was visited by one of the individuals that is sanctioned. It is a prosecutor, Katherine Harrington, who offered to improve the conditions of his detention in exchange for testimony which would incriminate Antonio Ledezma in a conspiracy against the government.

So these are just two recent pieces of information we have been made aware of just in the last few days that call to light the sort of human rights violations that are occurring in Venezuela. And I would encourage the State Department to take seriously, as this information comes in, because it gives us more and more people that we can look at for sanctions and also to shame them publicly.

One day we are going to have freedom in Venezuela. There will be a functional government again and hopefully a better future for the Venezuelan people, and these individuals responsible for the human rights abuses are going to have to be accountable for what they are doing. So that is why it is so critical that these human rights abuses be documented now so that in the future these individuals will be held to account for the crimes they are committing against the people of Venezuela.

Senator Kaine, I will leave you in charge while I go vote, and I will be back. So you probably have 10 minutes of questions.

Senator KAINE. I will easily occupy that, Mr. Chair. Thank you. And thanks to the witnesses and all.

The questions that I have been here to hear and your testimony I think has answered questions that I was going to ask about the internal situation in Venezuela and the relations of our sanctions to that situation and the human rights abuses.

I want to talk about the relationship of what is happening in Venezuela with neighbors, so in particular, Colombia, which is such a strong ally of the United States.

I was in Colombia in the middle of February, and I was actually there on a day when President Maduro came out with a fairly incendiary set of statements not only against the United States but also against Colombia. I mean, it just appeared, the classic situation where when things are going bad at home, find somebody else to blame. That he was blaming the United States did not strike me as that unusual. That is a classic page out of the playbook. But it was a little bit unusual I thought, the degree of some of the rhetoric that he was leveling against Colombia.

Now, that relationship is an important one. It is a complicated one. A lot of Venezuelans live in Colombia and vice versa. Venezuela has at times been sort of a haven for the FARC and at other times has helped advance the peace discussions between the Colombian Government and the FARC. Economic challenges in Venezuela could at an important time in Colombia, even kind of a fragile time in these negotiations, push folks across the borders in ways that would be destabilizing.

So I was just wondering, especially you, Mr. Lee, if you would talk about the situation in Venezuela now as it might affect Colombia, who has got to be one of our best partners in the world right now.

Mr. LEE. Well, I think one of the reasons why—of the three Foreign Ministers that UNASUR countries sent to Venezuela, one of them was the Foreign Minister of Colombia. And that reflects Colombia's important stake in what happens in Venezuela as a commercial partner, as a place, in the past, that had received large numbers of Colombians, and a preoccupation that has grown over time over what is going to be the impact of Venezuela's chronic mismanagement of its economy and how will that spill over into Colombia.

An additional element in all of this is the Colombian Government, particularly under President Santos, was greatly appreciative of the Venezuelan Government's support for the peace process in Colombia, which has been kind of a central focus of President Santos.

And so the various examples that you talked about highlight this cross-cutting sensitivity, and I think probably the best way of summarizing it is the Colombian Government is very conscious that if conditions continue to deteriorate in Venezuela, this will have an adverse and a direct adverse impact on Colombia. So that is one of the reasons why you have seen the Colombian Government trying to champion the region to focus along with Brazil and Ecuador. But in a sense, out of the three countries, what happens for good or bad in Venezuela has a far more direct impact on Colombia.

Senator KAINE. How do you interpret the statements of President Maduro kind of blasting Colombia for some of their own internal problems?

Mr. LEE. Well, President Santos like President Obama and Secretary Kerry is in good company because there is a certain theatrical element in the statements of President Maduro. The incident that you are referring to was basically President Santos coming to the defense of a former Colombian President that in his view had not been accorded with the respect due to a former Colombian President who was basically trying to demonstrate concern for the human rights of a key political prisoner.

Senator KAINE. This question may have been asked when I was over voting, out of the room. Talk a little bit about the current status of the situation with the reduction of U.S. Embassy personnel in Venezuela and how those discussions are ongoing with respect to the presence of Venezuela Embassy and consulate personnel in the United States.

Mr. LEE. We have proposed to the Venezuelan Government the need for bilateral discussions. We have proposed a team to meet with them so they can appreciate why we staff our mission the way they do and also for us to share with them how we see their staffing up here. Staffing in our respective diplomatic missions is essentially a function of what the host government agrees to and our operational requirements. And I think it is important for the Venezuelan Government to understand that we need a certain level of staffing in order to ensure the protection of our mission, in order to provide the level of consular services for Americans, and also to provide travel documents to Venezuelans who wish to come to the United States. Last year our Embassy in Caracas adjudicated 250,000 Venezuelan submissions for travel documents. We might not be able to support all of those functions if our staffing is reduced to certain numbers.

Senator KAINE. Mr. Smith, I would like to ask about the impacts of the sanctions thus far. Obviously, Venezuela is dealing with huge issues because of years of economic mismanagement, and then low oil prices themselves impose a significant cost on an economy that has really leaned heavily on that resource instead of having a more diverse economy. Talk a little bit about, to the extent that you can, what is the marginal effect of the sanctions from our side compared to the overall economic challenges, most of their own making, that Venezuela is dealing with.

Mr. SMITH. Thank you, Senator. I think one of the most important things to understand about the sanctions and to remember and that we emphasize is that these were targeted sanctions just against the seven individuals. So I think to the extent that it would affect Venezuela as a whole would be any kind of concern about the idea that we could do further sanctions with respect to the country there, I think our financial institutions in the United States and around the world may be a little bit more hesitant to deal with some of the potential bad actors in the Venezuelan society in the government because of the impact of the sanctions.

But one of the things that we also emphasize with these sanctions is they were not targeted at the Government of Venezuela. They were not targeted at the country of Venezuela, and they were not targeted at the people of Venezuela. So there has been the mix of—the impact—I think it would have been felt mostly on the individuals targeted and others that might believe they are to be targeted next.

Senator KAINE. And just kind of thinking down the road in terms of the strategic challenge you have in a situation like this, while some would say sanctions against just a few individuals, that is not showing the strength that they might want to see. Another argument would be, look, if there is an economic kind of collapse underway because of the mismanagement of the current government, to do bigger sanctions against the government would enable them to better say, oh, look, we are just having problems because the United States is doing bad things. Instead, by doing the sanctions against individuals, hopefully there would be more of an understanding among the Venezuelan population that the economic challenges they are facing are because of a government that is mismanaging the economy rather than because of the effect of the external sanctions. So I am kind of thinking through. That has to be, I guess, one of the balancing acts that you are using as you decide whether to make these sanctions just against individuals or against financial institutions or against the government itself. Am I correct in analyzing it that way?

Mr. SMITH. I can start. I would say, yes, you are right. I think one of the things that people do not recognize with sanctions is that more is not always better, that there could be some disadvantages to going out with the broad sanctions that would have significant disadvantages to the U.S. national security-foreign policy relationship not just with Venezuela but in the region. And so what we try to do is do the correct balance to make sure that in this case what we were doing was focusing on the bad actors, those that were undermining democratic institutions and that were abusing human rights. And the purpose of the sanctions—this first salvo was to actually show our concern with the human rights situation in Venezuela and really call attention to that.

Senator KAINE. Mr. Lee.

Mr. LEE. I would just add the action that we took against the seven—and we focused on seven very emblematic individuals who clearly had significant ties to human rights violations or corruption, and we were very confident in being able to highlight that. And that message was clearly heard.

But we believe that we need to combine a statement of principle and one of the ways of demonstrating those principles are the use of targeted sanctions against individuals but also trying to work, as best we can, with likeminded countries in the region to use their influence to try to help the Venezuelan opposition broker a relationship with the Venezuelan Government that would allow the political space for a credible electoral outcome in the next National Assembly elections. This particular message of working and trying to promote that discussion is much more effectively done by other countries than ourselves, and so we have to work somewhat indirectly through other countries to help that process.

So it is a combination of these statements of sanctions against specific individuals but this is all in the context of working collaboratively with likeminded countries in the region to try to influence the behavior of the Venezuelan Government.

Senator KAINE. We have been having, obviously, and will continue to have, significant discussions about Iran in this committee and in this chamber. Talk a little bit about the current Iranian-Venezuelan relationship, the degree of Iranian influence that you see in Venezuela these days.

Mr. LEE. Well, we are very vigilant about this particular relationship, which basically came into full fruition under previous Iranian and Venezuelan Presidents. Most parts of the agreements that have been reached by the two countries or statements have been mostly on economic or trade sets of issues. The overwhelming majority do not seem to have gone anywhere. Those joint ventures that have been established—we hear indirectly that lots of the Iranian companies complain of the conditions to operate in Venezuela like just about any other company finds itself in Venezuela.

But our particular attention is on Iranian activities, whether of their intelligence services or engaging in possible activities in money laundering or possible actions for avoiding sanctions on Iran. So these are all areas that we pay particularly close attention to on an ongoing basis.

So I would say, yes, this is a source of concern, and this is a relationship that we pay a lot of attention to.

Senator KAINE. And the last question I would like to ask is a little bit about Venezuela's influence in the region. Senator Gardner was, I think, being comical when he said the current Venezuelan leader had some of President Chavez's weaknesses but none of the charm. Clearly Venezuela was a regional player because of the strong personality of the previous leader but also because of the ability to use the resource of oil to win friends and influence people. Their own economic challenges have made that harder to do. Lower oil prices have complicated that situation, and I think the point that Senator Gardener was making that at least in terms of sort of the charismatic outreach to other nations, that is not the current President's strong suit. But that is my perception from afar.

Talk a little bit about Venezuela's ability to project influence in the Americas during this time of deepening economic crisis.

Mr. LEE. Well, I think Venezuela's ability to exercise influence has been gravely undermined by its serious economic problems and its ongoing efforts to try to stave off a balance of payments crisis. And you see this being played out in a variety of areas. Venezuela is unable to support Petrocaribe in a way that it had before. It has cut back significantly on some countries. Venezuela no longer can exercise the financial largesse that it could before. If anything, Venezuela is essentially staggering from one financial crisis to another trying to scrounge up enough money in order to pay for desperately needed imports for its population. And for the first time, we are hearing serious concerns about Venezuela's ability to have enough reserves to pay for food imports.

So all of these things conspire to basically put Venezuela very much on a defensive. It is one of the reasons for the Venezuelan Government trying ever so hard to obfuscate what is going on in Venezuela, to try to shed and put the blame on outside actors, of which we are only one. There are a variety of other countries or Presidential leaders from other countries that have been identified as doing a variety of imaginary bad things to Venezuela. So all of this is, I think, a reflection of the turmoil that Venezuela is finding itself.

Senator KAINE. And just kind of order of magnitude, you know, lower oil prices has been a very good thing for the world and for the United States generally. It does not mean every aspect of it is good. So Colombia, a great ally—lower oil prices hurts them. But they have a more diverse economy. Talk about oil revenues as a chunk of the Venezuelan economy or a chunk of the Venezuelan governmental budget. Give me an order of magnitude so that I can understand how much this drop and likely somewhat long-term low price is going to be affecting them.

Mr. LEE. Well, Venezuela depends—95 percent of its earnings from its oil sector. And chronic undercapitalization of its oil industry, wasteful government policies, price controls, labor controls, a three-tiered exchange system that puts a premium on insiders taking advantage of it, all of these have conspired to make the Venezuelan economy go into recession last year, even at a time when oil prices were about $100 a barrel. Now, with oil prices half of that, Venezuela is facing a really major foreign exchange problem. And Venezuela imports now far more than it did 10 years ago. So it imports virtually everything, all of its foodstuff, almost all of its consumer goods. And so you have seen kind of a progressive deterioration of Venezuelan companies to manufacture things because they cannot get the dollars necessary for the inputs to manufacture things in the country. And so that is one of the reasons why you are seeing widespread shortages and chronic shortages in the country.

Now with the drop of the oil prices to $50, that can only get infinitely worse. The IMF, for example, projects that Venezuela will suffer a contraction of 7 percent this year. Already the inflation rate is projected to go from 64 to over 80 percent. So we are dealing with a very chaotic Venezuelan economy and a Venezuelan Government that seems struggling to try to take any effective measures to arrest this downward economic slide.

Senator KAINE. And I just wanted to underline. I think I heard you right—kind of the statistic—95 percent of Venezuelan Government revenues are derived from the oil industry?

Mr. LEE. Yes, sir.

Senator KAINE. Last question. You know, talking about the prospects for a parliamentary or assembly—the legislative elections, again from afar, but just given the recent activity, the imprisonment of political opposition leaders, even some with significant posts, mayorships of major cities, the emergency decree entered into earlier in the month giving the President nearly complete power—I mean, you would have to be pessimistic. We got to keep pressing, but I mean, we should not be sugar-coating and suggesting that there is a high likelihood of elections that we will feel are free and fair. I mean, given all of the actions that are being undertaken right now, would not the prospects of elections that the global would look to be free and fair happening this year happening this year seem really, really slim?

Mr. LEE. Well, Senator, this is obviously a major concern of ours because we do see free and fair elections as a necessary first step for Venezuela to try to dig itself out of the situation it is in. And so that is the reason why we highlight the importance of these elections. We fully recognize and are concerned about President Maduro's acquisition of emergency decree powers. We will have to see how he utilizes those. But this is why we go to all of the countries in the region to emphasize that the region as a whole has an obligation to champion a democratic solution to Venezuela's problems.

Senator KAINE. I want to thank you both for your testimony. There is an ongoing vote, and so we will have a brief pause before the second panel is called up for their testimony. But to both of you, thank you very much. We will stand in a brief recess until the chair returns from voting, and then we will begin with the second panel. Thank you.

Excuse me. I excused you too soon. You almost got out the door. But I was informed that the chair may have some additional questions for the panel. There is a second vote and he is on his way back. So if you could just hang close before you are dismissed, but then we will move right into panel two. Thank you.

[Recess.]

Senator RUBIO. Thank you. I appreciate your patience. The committee will come back into order.

Members may come in and out. We just finished the second vote, so hopefully some folks will be able to make it back here. There are some other committee meetings going on as well.

Before I dismiss this panel, I appreciate your time and your patience indulging us here with these votes that are coming in.

Mr. Smith, I wanted to touch upon a couple issues with you in regards to the nature of this regime. So Ambassador Brownfield, the Assistant Secretary of the Bureau of International Narcotics and Law Enforcement Affairs, has been quoted as saying that recent media reports about the Venezuelan Government's complicity with cartels were not inconsistent with the evidence with regards to their work in drug trafficking.

And I wanted to share with you something that I hope we will continue to look at. Actually this is for both of you that I hope you will continue to look at.

There is a law enforcement advisory that went out in February of this year, and I want to read from it or paraphrase from it. But basically it said that there is reporting that indicates that government officials in Venezuela coordinate flights carrying bulk cash to the Syrian regime of Bashar al-Assad, that the source of these funds include funds that are donated by the Venezuelan Arab expatriate community, but the bulk of the cash includes money that Venezuelan officials collect for the trafficking of drugs and exacting bribes from other drug traffickers who land cash-loaded planes in Venezuela.

This, by the way, is part of a longer standing Venezuelan support of the Assad regime, as was reported back in 2012. The state-owned company, Petroleos de Venezuela, PDVSA, P-D-V-S-A—it was discovered that there were tankers in Syrian ports. This was discovered and disclosed, by the way, by an economic research firm that tracks maritime satellite data.

What do we know or what can any of you tell us about the links between the Maduro regime and the Government of Syria under Assad? Do we have any information on that you could share?

Mr. SMITH. I do not have any information I can share. We have been tracking the disturbing activities of members of the Government of Venezuela, and we have linked them publicly to narcotrafficking activities, and we have also linked them to other disturbing activities that we have been able to highlight in a variety regimes we have not designated pursuant to our Syria authorities.

Senator RUBIO. Well, this information again is produced by U.S. law enforcement agencies. They are obviously available to you. I would encourage you to look at them as we move forward. These are important pieces of information that we should not be ignoring and should certainly figure into our calculus.

There are also links to Iran and Venezuela. My office has received reports that there is a collusion between the Maduro regime and Argentina regarding an operation that could facilitate a transaction with Iran that would violate U.N. stipulations. Do you have any information on Venezuela providing Argentina with licit or illicit financial incentives in exchange for procuring Argentinean support toward this help toward Iran abating sanctions?

Mr. LEE. We are aware of those press reports and reports, but I have nothing to add to it at the moment.

Senator RUBIO. Okay. Well, there is a report by the Washington, DC-based Center for a Secure, Free Society and from Canada's Institute for Social and Economic Analysis which raises concerns about the use of Venezuela as a bridge to smuggle Iranian agents into North America. It states that Venezuelan authorities provided at least 173 passports, visas, and other documentation controlled by Cuba state-owned Albet to Islamist extremists seeking to slip unnoticed into North America. Have you followed up on those reports?

Mr. LEE. I have not. There may be others who have, but I am not in a position to comment on it.

Mr. SMITH. Senator, I would just add that we have sanctions investigators that work across our sanctions programs, including Iran, Syria narcotrafficking and now Venezuela, and they follow up on all of the law enforcement and intelligence reporting to try to build cases where they can.

Senator RUBIO. Now, I want to go through Venezuela's connection to Cuba. According to high-level military defectors from Venezuela's Government, there are between 2,700 and 3,000 Cuban intelligence agents in the South American nation embedded in sectors such as the military, agriculture, finance, and petroleum refining. According to high-level military defectors from Venezuela's Government, the Cubans have modernized Venezuela's intelligence services, both the SEBIN, which is the Bolivarian National Intelligence Service that reports directly to the President, and also military intelligence. They have also set up a special unit to protect Nicolas Maduro.

Last year, former Venezuelan intelligence agents and sources with direct access to active officers of the Bolivarian Armed Forces told El Nuevo Herald newspaper that Cuba plays a leading role in the repression unleashed by Maduro against Venezuelan protestors. The Cubans are in charge of operations which range from security around the Presidential palace to planning of arrests of opponents. These Venezuelan sources told El Nuevo Herald that Cubans have planned the operations of between 600 and 1,000 armed men who comprise the Chavista paramilitary group known as the colectivos.

In 2007, Juan Jose Rabilero, head of Cuba's Committee for the Defense of the Revolution, the CDR, very similar to the colectivos, claimed that there were over 30,000 members of Cuba's Committee for the Defense of the Revolution in Venezuela.

According to investigations by independent Venezuelan journalists, the Cubans have computerized Venezuela's public records giving them control over the issue of identity papers and voter registration. The Cubans have representatives in the ports and airports and have taken part in the purchases of military equipment. A state-owned Cuban company, Albet Ingenieria y Sistemas, received $170 million to develop electronic data systems in Venezuela. Through Albet, the Cuban Government has been given access to Venezuelan databases from which it can modify and even issue documents to citizens of other countries. Its portfolio includes the Maduro communications office and operating systems for prisons, emergency services, hospitals, and police.

Are you aware of the links between Venezuela and Cuba that go as deep as what I have just outlined, and if so, what have we done or are we doing to continue to monitor that and call attention to it?

Mr. LEE. Senator, the links between Cuba and Venezuela and the links between Cuba and Venezuela's intelligence services and military and a variety of other social missions is well known. Many of the things that you have said I am very familiar with. Some of them I am not. But the fundamental reality that there is a close relationship between both countries is very evident.

Senator RUBIO. Well, let me ask you this. You would agree that the Venezuelan Government under Maduro is repressing its own people. Right?

Mr. LEE. Yes.

Senator RUBIO. You would agree that the Cubans are helping the Venezuelans and putting in place the systems of repression.

Mr. LEE. I think that the kind of advice the Cubans provide is not necessarily the most democratic.

Senator RUBIO. Well, what does that mean? Are the Cubans helping the Venezuelans repress their own people? Are the Cubans assisting the colectivos, these armed groups, irregular groups on the ground that are used to confront protestors and other such activity?

Mr. LEE. I am personally not aware of a link between the Cubans and the colectivos. I am aware of the link between the colectivos and the use by the Maduro government of the colectivos to repress peaceful demonstrators. I think that is very clear.

Senator RUBIO. Are you aware that the Cubans are intricately involved in issuing documents in Venezuela such as voter registration, passports, and not just to Venezuelans but to noncitizens of Venezuela as well? Would you acknowledge that that is happening?

Mr. LEE. I am aware of some levels of cooperation that you are talking about.

Senator RUBIO. Mr. Lee, is Venezuela in your portfolio?

Mr. LEE. Yes, it is, sir.

Senator RUBIO. And the Cubans—everyone in Venezuela—in fact, anyone who looks at it realizes the Cubans are crawling all over the place in Venezuela. There are tens of thousands, perhaps hundreds of thousands of Cubans all over the country embedded in every sector of the government. I mean, anyone who comes back from Venezuela tells you that repeatedly. How can this be part of your portfolio and you not be aware of the enormous Cuban presence that exists in Venezuela?

Mr. LEE. Senator, I did not deny that Cuba has an outsized influence in Venezuela. It is clear that they have a long-standing and deep relationship in a variety of areas, including in the intelligence services, including in the military, including a wide variety of government agencies that we are perfectly aware of.

Senator RUBIO. So if you acknowledge that they have an outsized influence and they are involved in intelligence and security agencies, why can you not just state today what everyone knows, and that is that the Cuban Government is actively assisting the Venezuelan Government in suppressing its people?

That is what the Cubans are expert at in Venezuela. What else could they be contributing to the effort? That is what they are best known for on the island. That is what they have most established expertise at doing to their own people in Cuba. So you have a repressive regime in Cuba that for over 55 years has actively repressed its own people and cut down on all sorts of activity on the island. They have an outsized influence in Venezuela. They have an outsized influence in both its intelligence gathering and its security agencies. Why is that not a logical thing, even if you did not have specific facts, which I am sure you do, but even if we did not have it, why is it not a reasonable assumption that the Cubans are actively assisting the Venezuelan Government in suppressing the people of Venezuela?

Mr. LEE. The fundamental responsibility for what happens in Venezuela is the Venezuelan Government's. And really, if we are going to focus on where the blame is, it should be for the Venezuelan Government's own actions against its own people. And I think we need to focus on holding the Venezuelan Government responsible for its actions.

Senator RUBIO. No one disputes that, Mr. Lee, but the question is not whether the Venezuelans are ultimately responsible. Ultimately they are the ones that asked for the assistance and are putting it into place. The question is whether the Cubans are assisting the Venezuelan Government in putting in place the mechanisms that the Venezuelan Government is using to repress the people of Venezuela. You cannot answer that question today?

Mr. LEE. I think the Venezuelan Government charts its own course, takes advice from the Cubans on certain things, but fundamentally it is the Venezuelan Government that charts its own course, for good, for ill, whether effectively or feckless.

Senator RUBIO. Mr. Lee, I think what is obvious here is that you cannot say what everyone knows, and that is that the Cuban Government is helping the Venezuelan Government do this because, on the one hand, while we are sanctioning Venezuelan Government officials, we are lifting sanctions on Cuban officials that have made this possible. And so at the end of the day, it truly is amazing to me that in this hearing, the individual responsible for this portfolio on behalf of the U.S. Government refuses to state on the record that the Cuban Government is intricately involved in helping the Venezuelan Government to repress its own people.

This is a claim we have been willing to make about multiple countries around the world. This is a claim we have made about the Cubans in the past. This is a claim that we have made about the Cubans and that the State Department has acknowledged up until December of last year when suddenly they stopped talking about it.

I just find it unbelievable that we cannot get somebody from the Department of State who is responsible for this portfolio to openly acknowledge that the Cuban Government is providing extraordinary assistance to the Venezuelan Government in suppressing the people of Venezuela.

And I hope that you will reconsider. I hope the State Department will reconsider acknowledging that because it undermines our credibility as a nation to turn a blind eye to the role that the Cuban Government is playing in the suppression of the Venezuelan people.

The people of Venezuela are fully aware of it. There is not anyone that gets off a plane from Venezuela that does not tell you there are Cubans everywhere, and there are Cubans everywhere on the island involved in governmental functions. Multiple people from Venezuela will tell you that when you go get a passport or any document, it is oftentimes a Cuban behind the counter that is coordinating it all. And to somehow think they are there as a benign force for purposes of providing moral support is quite frankly absurd.

And so I hope that you will reconsider your answer in the days to come because it is clear to everyone who knows anything about this—and you know a lot about this—that the Cubans are helping the Venezuelans carry out these operations that they are taking against their own people.

With that, I think we are done with questions, and I appreciate both of you being here today.

We will call up our second panel.

Before we welcome the second panel, I would like to unanimous consent that a letter by Ms. Maria Eugenia Tovar, who is the mother of Genesis Carmona Tovar, who was murdered by a gunshot on February 18, 2014, while participating at a peaceful demonstration in Venezuela be included in the record.

Now, let me welcome the panel. Douglas Farah is the president of IBI Consultants and a senior (non-resident) associate of the Americas Program at the Center for Strategic and International Studies. He works as a consultant and subject-matter expert on security challenges, terrorism, and transnational organized crime in Latin America both for the U.S. Government and the private sector.

Santiago Canton is an executive director of Partners for Human Rights at the Robert F. Kennedy Center for Justice and Human Rights. Mr. Canton manages programs around the globe that promote and protect human rights and strengthen democratic processes through strategic litigation, capacity building, and advocacy initiatives.

Dr. Christopher Sabatini is the senior director of policy at the Americas Society and Council of the Americas and founder and editor in chief of the hemispheric policy magazine, Americas Quarterly. Dr. Sabatini chairs the AS/COA Rule of Law Working Group. He has served as an advisor to the World Bank and the U.S. Agency for International Development.

I welcome all three of you here, and I will begin with you, Dr. Sabatini.

STATEMENT OF CHRISTOPHER SABATINI, PH.D., ADJUNCT PROFESSOR, SCHOOL OF INTERNATIONAL AND PUBLIC AFFAIRS AT COLUMBIA UNIVERSITY, NEW YORK, NY

Dr. SABATINI. First of all, thank you, Senator for the invitation. Thank you also for your dedicated commitment to speaking out on human rights violations in Venezuela and your commemoration just recently of the start of the peaceful protests a year ago, and of course, the legislation that led to the Executive orders.

I am going to talk about three things today. The first is the political and economic situation in Venezuela. The second is the very sad lack of a regional response to the deterioration in that situation. And the last is the recent U.S. Executive orders that came and caused such a commotion, if you will, in the region.

First, the political and economic situation in Venezuela. As all of the people said, it is likely to get worse. Sixteen years of economic mismanagement and incompetence have wreaked havoc on the Venezuelan economy. There is greater concentration in the economy on oil—it now represents 95 of exports—and lower productivity of that oil. In addition there is a huge public sector deficit. There are over $8 billion the Venezuelan Government will have to pay to foreign creditors this year alone, with only about $20 billion in the central bank. And according to different estimates, oil has to be anywhere between $100 to $120 per barrel to be able to meet the government's expectations when, of course, it is around $50 a barrel.

The IMF, as you mentioned, Senator, is expecting contraction of the economy this year of 7 percent on top of the contraction of 2.8 percent, and in addition to the inflation rates we have talked about, people are now actually saying by the end of this year, inflation may reach triple digits.

What makes this worse is the level of political confrontation. At every turn when things have gotten worse with this government, people hope and expect it to moderate, whether it was when Chavez lost a referendum or whether it was the close election with Maduro who only won by about 1.5 percent of the vote, people thought he could follow a more moderate course. He did not. When the going gets tough, he confronts, and that has been precisely the problem. And I expect because of that, the economic and political situation will get worse, which brings me to the regional response.

Despite multiple commitments among multilateral organizations to defend and protect human rights, the regional community in Venezuela has been mute. What that means is by standing aside as this President disarticulates democratic institutions, attacks political opponents and jails mayors, the regional community has been an enabler to the violation of human rights in Venezuela. That has to be recognized. They are violating their own commitments to a number of multilateral organizations.

The only voices that have spoken up are Juan Manuel Santos, the President of Colombia, and five former Presidents who signed a letter just last week expressing their concern about the confrontation, including Oscar Arias Sanchez, including former President Zedillo, Calderon, and Fernando Henrique Cardoso.

Which brings to the Executive order. It is important to distinguish, as everyone has so far, that these are only very targeted sanctions against people. Unfortunately, the language that was used as a result bureaucratic boilerplate became a red herring. But what is really sad about this is that in 2009 the United States pulled the visas of 15 Honduran officials of the de facto government of Micheletti. At that time, they did not use the language they are using now of calling it intervention or impertinent intervention in the internal affairs of a country and respecting national sovereignty. They applauded that decision. I think it is worth asking regional leaders in the hemisphere why is it okay to pull visas of a de facto government that came to power in a coup in Honduras, but why are they not willing to stand by the United States when it does the exact same thing in Venezuela. And what is wrong with allowing a government to be able to say to human rights abusers we do not want you to come to Disneyland? We do not want you to do your banking in our—again, I would like to say that I think this is a very, very sad moment in terms of the regional commitment to democracy which has eroded when only 15 years ago they stood up collectively and denounced violations, the very same violations by Alberto Fujimori and rolled them back?

I am also concerned about the way the media has portrayed this. Again, the language around the Executive order was problematic, but the media has presented this as giving Maduro steam, as giving him sort of bait to be able to roll back democratic institutions and build political momentum. The truth is that is not true. His disapproval rating still stands at 70 percent, and his approval rating still stands at 23 percent. In other words, this has not become a political boon to the President, but yet, regional leaders and the media insist on that it is.

I will end on one last point. While the language about Venezuela—national security risk may have been a little overblown, I would argue that it is a security risk in the region. For the first time, we face the specter of a failed state in a large South American country just south of us, and that is unprecedented. And getting out of it and how you would rebuild eventually is unimaginable.

[The prepared statement of Dr. Sabatini follows:]

PREPARED STATEMENT OF DR. CHRISTOPHER SABATINI

The confluence of Venezuela's fast deteriorating economy, the increased targeting of political opponents, the National Assembly's granting decree powers to President Nicolas Maduro, and the mobilization of the military make it impossible to predict what will happen for the remainder of Maduro's term, which ends in 2019. As things stand today, though, it's impossible to see this ending well.

I say this for four reasons.

First, 16 years of severe economic mismanagement—public fiscal profligacy; the economy's greater concentration on oil exports (which now represent 95 of the country's exports); pervasive corruption; a complicated, severely overvalued exchange rate; and the arbitrary expropriation of select industries—combined now with the drastic drop in the price of oil (to under $50 a barrel)—have left the country teetering on the brink of an economic meltdown. The International Monetary Fund (IMF) has predicted that Venezuela's GDP will contract by 7 percent this year, after contracting by more than 2 percent last year and inflation is hovering around 70 percent, though most now believe it will reach triple digits by the end of the year. And the stories of shortages of basic foods and goods are well known. People are suffering economically, and it will only increase.

Second, in the 16 years that the Bolivarian Revolution has been in power, it has systematically taken apart the checks and balances of democratic government and politicized the state. This has included packing the judicial system (including the supreme court) and the electoral commission with political allies, tearing down the independence of the Central Bank, closing down or buying out independent media, creating parallel local governments and police forces, cracking down on political opponents—including one former mayor, Leopoldo Lopez, who has been in prison for more than 1 year and the mayor of Caracas, Antonio Ledezma, who was jailed earlier this month—and politicizing the armed forces.

More than just a violation of fundamental democratic principles, what has occurred is that the very institutions that would be necessary to mediate political disputes and manage conflict have become completely vitiated and distrusted by a large portion of the population.

Which brings me to the third point, this government—both that of former President Hugo Chavez and his successor Maduro—has never shown any tendency to moderate. If anything, when faced with difficulty and adversity, their reaction has been the opposite: to double down on their policies and pursue a more confrontational strategy. That tendency has become more pronounced and worsened under Maduro, who, even as the country clearly veers toward economic collapse and faces broad popular protests, answers by toughening his position: cracking down on opponents, blaming others—the opposition, economic elites and, of course, the United States—and accumulating more power under the executive and for the party, the United Social Party of Venezuela (PSUV). This does not appear likely to change, and will—as it has—only worsen the country's economy and its political divisions.

Fourth, despite multiple multilateral commitments to defend human rights and representative democracy the regional community has been practically mute on this issue. Venezuela's neighbors, such as Brazil, Argentina, Bolivia, Ecuador, and Chile, have shown no inclination to become involved to defend basic human rights and democratic norms. There was a brief effort last year by the South American Union (UNASUR) to try to mediate the dispute between the government and the political opposition after street protests had swept the country over political and economic conditions, resulting in more than 40 dead and the arrest of three opposition leaders, including Leopoldo Lopez. Those efforts at mediation produced nothing, Perhaps worse—I would argue—they were conducted under a value-neutral calculus. Rather than attempting to defend the right of peaceful democratic protests and secure the release of what were clearly politically motivated arrests, the South American Union's delegation intervened to mediate the dispute, treating both sides as moral equals.

By standing aside as the Maduro government attacks democratic institutions and the opposition, the regional community has enabled the violation of human rights of Venezuelan citizens. The lack of effective collective action has not only allowed the conditions in Venezuela to fester, they have loosened the region's overall commitment to democratic standards. The question is who will stand up? Unfortunately, other than Colombian President Juan Manuel Santos' statement after the arrest of Antonio Ledezma and the other mayors, no sitting President has—though four former Presidents Fernando Henrique Cardoso of Brazil, Oscar Arias of Costa Rica, Alejandro Toledo of Peru, and Ernest Zedillo and Felipe Calderon of Mexico recently wrote a letter public letter expressing their concern.

Perhaps even more curious, the countries of the South American Union issued a statement after President Barack Obama's Executive order to pull the visas of seven Venezuelan public officials and froze their assets, criticizing the action.

Which brings me to the last point on the White House and Treasury Department's Executive order last week.

Unfortunately, the language calling Venezuela a national security risk to the U.S. that accompanied the announcement revoking the visas of the seven officials and freezing any assets they may have in the U.S. has become a red herring, provoking a ridiculous ramping up of military preparedness of Venezuelan troops for an imaginary U.S. invasion, justifying a power grab by Maduro for decree powers and even provoking South American nations through UNASUR to denounce the policies.

A few clarifying points are in order, though.

First, the Executive order was only to pull the visas of these officials, basically denying them the right to travel to the United States. These are not sanctions on the country or sanctions on the general population. They are an effort to deny those who were involved in human rights abuses from entering the U.S. territory. Dare I ask, what's wrong with denying human rights abusers the right to travel to your country?

Second, there has emerged an unremarked contrast between Latin American reactions to the denial of Venezuelan Government officials U.S. visas and their reactions to a similar U.S. action in 2009 on officials in Honduras. In the summer of 2009, the U.S. pulled the visas of 15 high-level officials of the de facto government of then-President Roberto Micheletti. Far from calling it ''an interventionist threat to the principle of non-interference in the internal affairs of other countries'' (the language used by the South American Union last week), the U.S. decision was applauded by the regional community. Today, it is being denounced as impertinent intervention. Why? Either sympathies toward the target government are different or the region has changed. I suspect both, but in either case it smacks of hypocrisy from our partners in the hemisphere, and a egregious betrayal of Venezuelan citizens' human rights

Third, it was the absence of action from regional partners that prodded the U.S. to action. Whatever you may think of the actions the U.S. took, they have occurred in a vacuum when the Venezuelan Government's actions only 15 years ago would have provoked expressions of concern and even action among elected governments in the region. Today, it is only the former, elected, democratic Presidents that I mentioned earlier who are willing to speak up. But clearly Venezuela's teetering economy and human rights situation are a immediate regional issue that demands a regional response.

Which brings me to my last point. While Venezuela doesn't represent a national security risk to the U.S. in the alarmist way hinted at in last week's Executive order, it is a risk, more regional perhaps, but a risk.

For one, the disarticulation of institutions and the politicization of the state described above, given the economic and political crisis the country finds itself, raise the specter of a failed state in the Western Hemisphere. This level of economic calamity and lack of institutionality has not existed in a major Latin American country/economy in recent history. The question of how to end this downward spiral and rebuild the country is unprecedented . . . not to mention unimaginable.

Then there are also the well substantiated allegations of the Venezuelan state's involvement in narcotics trafficking. Evidence has grown that segments of the country's armed forces, including the National Guard, and elected officials are involved in transporting cocaine from Colombia and money laundering. Regarding the latter, the recent case opened up by the U.S. Treasury Department accusing the Banco Popular de Andorra of laundering $4.2 billion points to the level of corruption and nefarious activities occurring in Venezuela today. Are we to believe that the government isn't aware of this?

One need only look at the map of flights ferrying cocaine from South America to northern markets in which Venezuela is arched with overflights or dotted with take off points to see the central place the Andean country has taken in the drug trade. With the three countries that border it (Colombia, Guyana, and Brazil), numerous countries affected by its alleged role in narcotrafficking, and Venezuela teetering on economic and political collapse, Venezuela would seem to be more of a risk to regional security than to the United States.

Unfortunately, Venezuela's neighbors have chosen to focus on a hyperbolic U.S. statement rather than how the looming crisis in the country could affect them and their responsibility and role to prevent it.

Senator RUBIO. Thank you. Thank you, Dr. Sabatini.
Mr. Canton.

STATEMENT OF SANTIAGO CANTON, EXECUTIVE DIRECTOR, PARTNERS FOR HUMAN RIGHTS, ROBERT F. KENNEDY CENTER FOR JUSTICE AND HUMAN RIGHTS, WASHINGTON, DC

Mr. CANTON. Thank you very much, Mr. Chairman, for the opportunity to appear before you today to share some information regarding the human rights situation in Venezuela. I have presented a 20-page written statement with very detailed information about the human rights situation. So in this brief presentation, I will just refer to the most important violations.

The rule of law in Venezuela has been in a downward spiral for the last 15 years. The signs of this decline have been unequivocal: increasing concentration of power; lack of independence of the judiciary; restricting freedom of expression; excessive and lethal use of force and other forms of restrictions to peaceful assembly; widespread use of torture; restricting civic space and financing of NGOs; and prosecuting under false charges political opposition leaders; and closing the door to any outside monitoring.

Violations for freedom of expression. Journalists face constant threats and harassment. The state exercises tight control of our media outlets and has been ranked 137 out of 180 countries in the 2015 World Press Freedom Index. The U.N. Secretary General, the High Commissioner of Human rights of the U.N., and the Special Rapporteur on the Right to Freedom of Opinion and Expression of the U.N. have criticized the Venezuelan Government for limiting free expression. Over 259 incidents of threats and harassment of journalists were reported between January and April 2014.

In recent years, state authorities have tightened restrictions on television and radio through forced closures, fines, judicial cases, and economic pressures. From 2013 to 2014, 13 newspapers stopped operating and many more are at risk of closure now due to print paper shortages that the government is responsible for.

Violations to freedom of association and assembly. Peaceful opposition protestors are routinely violently assaulted by the Venezuelan police and military, the latter of which was recently granted explicit power to use force to control peaceful demonstrations. Law prohibits Venezuelan human rights defenders from receiving international support if they defend political rights or monitor the performance of public bodies. Protests have reignited since last February of this year. Violent repression and the use of military force during these demonstrations have already resulted in a fatal victim. On February 24, Kluiverth Roa Nunez, a 14-year-old high school student, was killed by a gunshot to the head.

Lack of judicial independence. Since the National Assembly passed a law that increased the membership of the Supreme Court from 20 to 32 justices, its members have publicly rejected the principle of separation of powers and the judiciary has acted as another arm of the executive branch to advance the government's political agenda.

Arbitrary arrests and detentions. According to the Office of the High Commissioner of Human rights of the U.N., more than 70 people have been arbitrarily detained or arrested in Venezuela over the last year alone. According to official information, approximately 3,000 people were arrested between February and June 2014 in the context of the public protests that took place across the country. Many were denied access to a lawyer, and some remained in pretrial detention for several months. Dozens of students remain also in detention.

One of the individuals that were arrested in connection to the February 2014 protests is Leopoldo Lopez, leader of the opposition party, Voluntad Popular. He has remained in pretrial detention with fabricated charges.

A month after, the mayor of San Cristobal, Daniel Ceballos, from the same party was also arrested.

In August 2014, the U.N. Working Group on Arbitrary Detentions concluded that the detention of both Lopez and Ceballos was arbitrary and demanded its release. Recently a couple of months ago, the Committee Against Torture of the U.N. also demanded the release of them.

One year after Leopoldo Lopez's arrest, Caracas Mayor Antonio Ledezma, the second most-voted person in Venezuela after Maduro, was also arrested on fabricated charges.

Torture and cruel, inhumane and degrading treatment in prisons. The U.N. Committee Against Torture expressed alarm regarding reported acts of torture and ill-treatment of persons arrested in connection with the demonstrations of February of last year. These acts of torture include beatings, electric shocks, burns, suffocation, sexual violence, and threats.

Just earlier this month, the Inter-American Commission of Human rights granted protective measures in favor of two political prisoners in ''the tomb'' prison that you referred to, Senator. It is important to note that these type of measures are only granted in extreme cases of urgency, gravity, and threats of irreparable harms.

Then there is the violation of political participation. I am running out of time, so I am going to finish very quickly with this presentation.

There is a violation of the right to political participation. As you know, Leopoldo Lopez was not allowed to run in the election, and in addition to Leopoldo Lopez, just recently Julio Borges, another member of the opposition, was also expelled from Congress. Maria Corina Machado was expelled a few months ago. So it is very difficult for the opposition to participate freely in politics.

Mr. Chairman, the disregard by the Venezuelan Government of the human rights of its people is absolute. The human rights situation in Venezuela is critical and not only for opposition leaders but for the population in general. The report by the U.N. Committee Against Torture from last December indicates that almost 1,300— and I insist, 1,300—extrajudicial killings took place in Venezuela between 2012 and 2013. And the prevailing impunity does not contribute to improve the situation. According to government information, of the approximately 30,000 human rights violations reported to the authorities between 2011 and 2014, only 3 percent have been prosecuted.

The account I have just presented is only but a fraction of the grave and systematic violations that are taking place in Venezuela. It is time for the international community to ensure through multilateral and bilateral efforts that democracy and the rule of law are respected. In 2001, the hemisphere adopted the Democratic Charter to address challenges such as the ones Venezuela is going through. The U.S. Government should work together with the OAS and UNASUR and the leaders of the region to ensure that the Democratic Charter is respected.

Thank you very much.

[The prepared statement of Mr. Canton follows:]

PREPARED STATEMENT OF SANTIAGO A. CANTON

Chairman Rubio, Ranking Member Boxer, and members of the Subcommittee on the Western Hemisphere, thank you for the opportunity to appear before you today to share critical information impacting United States policy toward Venezuela, in particular regarding the human rights and security situation in that country. I commend the committee for holding this important and timely hearing.

INTRODUCTION

Democracy and rule of law in Venezuela have been on a downward spiral for the past 15 years, with great consequences not only for the country's economy and security, but also for the human rights of the Venezuelan people. I would like to focus on this generalized disregard for the respect of basic human rights that has become the state-sanctioned rule in Venezuela.

The signs of this decline have been unequivocal: increasing concentration of power in the executive branch, debilitating the independence and autonomy of the judiciary; restricting freedom of expression and shutting down dissenting media outlets; excessive—sometimes lethal—use of force and other forms of restrictions to peaceful assembly; widespread use of torture and horrid detention conditions; restricting civic space and financing of NGOs; imposing administrative sanctions or even prosecuting under false charges political opposition leaders; and closing the door to any outside monitoring or criticism, among others.

The current human rights violations in Venezuela are not isolated instances. On the contrary, they are the product of a pattern of systematic violations that started more than a decade ago. To understand what is currently happening in Venezuela it is necessary to know the context that gives rise to today's violations. Instead of reversing this trend, the assumption of power by Nicolas Maduro after president Chavez's death has only increased the government's repression of the Venezuelan people in a desperate attempt to hold on to power in the midst of growing popular discontent.

Chavez and Maduro have repeatedly disregarded all the accusations of human rights violations as an international conspiracy of right wing individuals and NGOs. However, respected institutions and groups of the international community have consistently denounced the human rights violations taking place in Venezuela.

International human rights bodies and officials, including the United Nations High Commissioner for Human Rights, the U.N. Special Rapporteur on Torture, the Working Group on Arbitrary Detention, the U.N. Rapporteur on Extrajudicial Executions, the U.N. Special Rapporteur on the independence of judges and lawyers and the U.N. Special Rapporteur on Human Rights Defenders, as well as regional bodies such as the Inter-American Commission and Inter-American Court of Human Rights, have made strong calls of concern over the last years regarding the intentional disregard by the Venezuelan Government of its human rights obligations under international law.

Openness to dissent and criticism has not only been lacking with regard to local actors. In fact, since 1996 no special procedure of the United Nations has been allowed to visit the country.[1] Likewise, there have been several instances of international human rights delegations of nongovernmental organizations being expelled from the country, including a Human Rights Watch's delegation.[2]

Widespread human rights abuses are committed daily in total impunity. The Venezuelan Government itself admits the shockingly low levels of violations that end up being prosecuted. In its most recent reports to the U.N. Committee Against Torture, the government informed the committee that of the 31,096 human rights violations reported to the authorities between 2011 and 2014, only in 3.1 percent did a prosecutor present criminal charges.[3]

Meanwhile, the government continues amassing authority and completely eroding the separation of powers. Indeed, since 2010 the Government has adopted a series of so-called Enabling Laws (Leyes Habilitantes), which authorize the President of the Republic to issue decrees with the rank, value, and force of statute on those matters that are so delegated. Many of these laws are overly broad and have been used by the Executive to imposed restrictions on human rights without appropriate controls. Following his predecessor's steps, just a few months after assuming power, President Maduro requested the National Assembly to enact a law granting him special powers for 12 months to address the economy and combat corruption. On November 19, 2013, a law was passed which allow the President to reform—by decree—norms to strengthen punishment in criminal, administrative, civil and disciplinary areas ''to avoid damage to or inadequate management of the public patrimony, and to prevent acts of corruption'' and norms that punish "attacks on the Security and Defense of the Nation, the institutions of the State, Public Powers, and the provision of public services indispensable to the development and the quality of life of the people"; among other areas generally reserved to Congress.[4] On Sunday, February 15, the National Assembly started discussing a new "Enabling law" requested by President Maduro to receive special decree powers for at least the next 6 months, allegedly in response to the most recent U.S. sanctions.[5]

Authorities at several levels openly disregard the Venezuelan Constitution, as has been recently the case with the Minister of Defense's authorization to the armed forces to potentially use lethal force if needed to control public protests.[6] This authorization to use lethal force is even more concerning taking into consideration the existing pattern of extrajudicial executions that has taken place in Venezuela over the last decade. According to information collected by the U.N. Committee Against Torture, 667 homicides at the hands of state agents were committed in 2012 and 600 in 2013.[7]

While openly restricting civil and political rights, the government of Venezuela has also made an effort to portray itself as a promoter of economic, social and cultural rights both domestically and throughout the region by providing economic assistance through Petrocaribe [8] and other foreign assistance programs. Indeed, in June 2013, Venezuela received recognition from the United Nations Food and Agriculture Organization (FAO) for the early achievement of one of the Millennium Development Goals and the World Food Summit (WFS) goal of halving the number of hungry people by 2015.[9] However, there have been growing reports over the past few years on the increasing difficulties for the Venezuelan population to access food and other basic necessities,[10] which President Maduro attributes to "an economic war by sectors who seek to destabilize the country . . . through the undersupply of food products."[11]

This situation has motivated a series of measures against private distributorships of food and other basic supplies, including the adoption in 2011 of the Law on Costs and Fair Prices that regulates a "maximum" sales price for certain foods and other goods.[12] Such measures have included, in extreme cases, taking over a toilet paper factory,[13] the authorization to occupy supermarket chain accused of "hoarding" and more recently, putting Venezuela's food distribution under military protection.[14]

MAJOR HUMAN RIGHTS VIOLATIONS

I. Violations of Freedom of Expression

Violations of the right to freedom of expression are rampant in Venezuela. Journalists face constant threats and harassment. The State exercises tight control over media outlets, including through restrictive telecommunications laws. There is overall repression of dissenting views. Peaceful protesters are violently attacked. A review of the analysis of leading human rights and press freedom organizations reveal a shockingly bad situation.

The United Nations Secretary General, High Commissioner for Human Rights, and Special Rapporteur on the promotion and protection of the right to freedom of opinion and expression have strongly criticized the Venezuelan Government for severely limiting free expression in the country, and have urged authorities "to ensure that people are not penalized for exercising their rights to peaceful assembly and freedom of expression."[15]

Venezuelan media outlets are governed by the 2004 Law on Social Responsibility in Radio, Television, and Electronic Media (Resorte), amended in 2010. CONATEL has used this law to impose heavy fines on television and print media outlets, which have criticized the government.[16] It is also through this law that the Venezuelan Government gave itself the authority to require all broadcasters to air the obligatory broadcasts previously mentioned.[17]

Furthermore, changes to the Organic Law of Telecommunications in December 2010 declared broadcast media and the Internet to be public services reserved for the State. These changes gave the Venezuelan Executive the power to suspend and revoke broadcasting concessions and to take control over privately owned stations or channels whose operating licenses were allowed to expire or were terminated.[18]

In recent years, State authorities have gradually tightened restrictions on television and radio through forced closures, fines, judicial cases, and economic pressures.[19] The most famous examples of this trend are with regard to Venezuela's oldest private television channel, Radio Caracas Television (RCTV), and main opposition channel, Globovision. In May 2007, the Government of Venezuela decided not to renew RCTV's license, forcing it to close down. Globovision was taken over in 2010 and then sold to pro-government owners in 2013, essentially eliminating the primary media voice critical of the Chavez and Maduro governments.

Numerous other media outlets have been forced to shut down because of government pressure as well. Various sources reported the closure of 34 radio stations in 2009 and 27 in 2011. From 2013 to 2014, 13 newspapers stopped operating according to El Nacional[20] and many more are at risk of closure now due to newsprint shortages. The Venezuelan Government has decreed that media organizations can only import newspaper if it is purchased with dollars provided through government currency exchange, but independent media sources are systematically denied this option.[21]

The Venezuelan Government also continues to use "obligatory national radio and television broadcasts to transmit government messages," according to information received by Inter-American Commission on Human Rights.[22]

In response to the February 2014 protests, the IACHR issued a press release in which it noted with concern the fact that CONATEL, the Venezuelan National Telecommunications Commission, had issued an official statement in which it advised media outlets that coverage of the protest-related violence could be considered a violation of the Resorte Law, for which they would be sanctioned accordingly.[23] The Special Rapporteur on Freedom of Expression expressed particular concern at the continuing and worsening pattern of government actions resulting in the loss of opportunities for public debate, noting the lack of guarantees for the free and independent exercise of the right to freedom of expression in conformity with Venezuela's international obligations.[24]

Since 2003 and continuing until today, Freedom House, an independent watchdog organization dedicated to the expansion of freedom around the world, has rated Venezuela as "not free" given that "the ability of independent journalists and media outlets to operate freely and impartially" has been seriously impeded by the political and economic crises which have evolved under the leadership of Hugo Chavez and Nicolas Maduro.[25] In its most recent analysis, it states that "Maduro's administration hampered the opposition media by arbitrarily fining outlets, enforcing licensing requirements without respecting due process rights, and excluding certain outlets from access to public information."[26] Furthermore, "high-level government officials constantly demonized opposition-aligned outlets and exerted systematic pressure on the tone and content of reporting."[27] Human Rights Watch has likewise noted with grave concern that "over the past decade, the [Venezuelan] government has expanded and abused its powers to regulate media."[28]

Reporters without Borders has also expressed its grave concern at the rapidly eroding press freedoms in Venezuela, and has ranked it 137 out of 180 countries on the 2015 World Press Freedom Index.[29] This marks a significant decline from its ranking of 116 in 2014, and demonstrates the continued and rapid deterioration of press freedoms in Venezuela.[30] The organization notes that "local and foreign journalists were the targets of threats, insults, physical attacks, theft, destruction of equipment and arrests during a succession of protests" and places the blame for the majority of these with the Bolivarian National Guard.[31]

The Committee to Protect Journalists details the shutting down of critical radio and television stations, the shortage of newsprint as the government seeks to control imports, and the resignations of multiple journalists who have complained of censorship.[32] The CPJ characterizes these actions on the part of the Venezuelan Government as "a campaign to silence the critical media."[33]

With regards to threats and harassment of journalists, over 259 incidents between January and April 2014 were reported to the U.N. Committee Against Torture.[34] The Venezuelan National Association of Journalists reported more than 50 incidents of violence or threats against reporters between 12 and 21 February 2014 alone.[35]

In its 2013 annual report, the Special Rapporteur on Freedom of Expression of the Inter-American Commission on Human Rights, published details of the almost 80 reports it received during the previous year of threat and assaults of journalists.[36] Likewise, the Commission compiled information on almost 40 attacks on newspaper offices and radio stations during the same time period.[37] In a September 2014 press release, the Commission once again called on the Government of Venezuela to respect the right to freedom of expression, citing reports that President Maduro had publicy accused CNN en Espanol, El Nuevo Herald, NTN24, and other media outlets of engaging in "media terrorism."[38]

In the Case of *Perozo et al.* v. *Venezuela*, the Inter-American Court of Human Rights considered a series of attacks against and harassment of Globovision Television Channel staff, including hostile public remarks and physical and verbal attacks by state officials. The State was found to have violated its obligations under the American Convention on Human Rights to "ensure the right to freely seek, receive ad impart information and the right to humane treatment."[39] Despite this judgment, Globovision would ultimately succumb to pressure and fall under State control, as detailed below.

II. Violations to freedom of association and assembly

Examples of violations of the rights to freedom of association and assembly are also abundant. Peaceful opposition protesters are routinely violently assaulted by the Venezuelan police and military, the latter of which was recently granted explicit power to use force to control peaceful demonstrations.[40] Indeed, on January 27, 2015, the Minister of Defense authorized the use of "potentially lethal force, be it with a firearm or with another potentially lethal weapon" as a last recourse [. . .], "to avoid public disorder, to support the legitimate authority, and to immediately reject aggression using any necessary means,"[41] in direct contradiction with article 68 of the Venezuelan Constitution, which explicitly prohibits the use of firearms and toxic substances as a means of containing public protests.

A legal framework has been put in place that has incrementally more severely restricted freedom of association and assembly in Venezuela. For example, under the Law for the Defense of Political Sovereignty and National Self-Determination, passed in 2010, Venezuelan human rights defenders are prohibited from receiving international support. As Human Rights Watch noted in a December 2010 press release, the law bars Venezuelan NGOs "that 'defend political rights' or 'monitor the performance of public bodies'" from receiving money from foreign sources.[42] Furthermore, the law permits the expulsion of foreigners invited by NGOs "if they express opinions that 'offend the institutions of state, top officials or attack the exercise of sovereignty.'"[43] Venezuelan civil society organizations liaising with foreign donors would also be sanctioned, facing high fines and individual prohibitions against running for public office.[44] Under the "Organic Law on Social Control," adopted by the National Assembly at the same time, individuals are obligated to adhere to Venezuela's socialist principles and values or face civil, administrative, or criminal sanctions.[45] Both of these laws aggressively limit the activities of human rights defenders.

The International Center for Not-for-Profit Law, for its part, has also detailed the dire legal situation in which Venezuelan civil society finds itself. It characterizes the enactment of the laws mentioned thus far, as well as Decree No. 458, which created the Strategic Center of Security and Protection of the Country (CESPPA), as having an overall chilling effect on freedom of assembly.[46] Opposition leaders have concluded that the goal of CESPPA is to control and censor the worsening political, economic, and social crisis enveloping the country.[47]

Even prior to the passage of these laws, in its 2009 Annual Report, the Inter-American Commission on Human Rights noted a "trend toward the use of criminal charges to punish people exercising their right to demonstrate or protest against government policies."[48] During the 5 years prior to the publication of that report, the Inter-American Commission received information regarding 2,200 individuals who faced criminal charges in connection with their involvement in public demonstrations.[49] These crimes, which include "blocking public highways, resisting the authorities, damage to public property, active obstruction of legally established institutions, offenses to public officials, criminal instigation and criminal association, public incitement to law-breaking, conspiracy, restricting freedom of employment, and breaches of the special secure zones regime, among others, carry prison sentences of up to 20 years.[50] More recently, Freedom House and PROVEA (Programa Venezolano de Educacion-Accion en Derechos Humanos) have echoed the concerns of the Inter-American Commission, reporting that at least 10 protesters were put on trial before military courts in 2012.[51]

The same groups have tracked the continually increasing repression of peaceful protests in Venezuela. According to Freedom House, "PROVEA described a sharp rise in suppressed protests in 2007, including a 300-percent increase in the number of injuries sustained during demonstrations, many caused by beatings, rubber bullets, and tear gas. The group also reported a 250-percent increase in the number of cases in which charges were brought against protesters, a sign of the ongoing criminalization of protest."[52]

The use of force by law enforcement during a protest must be considered in the context of the human rights to freedom of association and assembly. The principal purpose of a law enforcement presence at demonstrations should be to ensure public safety and protect the rights of protesters and bystanders.[53] The use of force by police is only permissible if it is strictly or absolutely necessary to protect an individual from harm or to enable a lawful arrest,[54] not for the purpose of infringing upon a protester's right to freedom of assembly and association. Use of force must be strictly necessary and proportional to the danger to the physical integrity or life of the law enforcement agent or other individual.[55] Whenever the lawful use of force is unavoidable, it must minimize damage to property and injury to persons, and respect and preserve human life.[56] Furthermore, law enforcement must ensure that medical aid is rendered to any injured protesters and that their next of kin are notified.[57]

Despite these internationally recognized principles, Venezuelan authorities have deployed excessive use of force against protesters in violation of multiple human rights, including the rights to freedom of assembly and association. At the outbreak of violence against protesters in February 2014, the Inter-American Commission on Human Rights declared that it was "profoundly disturbed by various complaints alleging violations of the demonstrators' rights to peaceful protest and their rights to life and humane treatment, personal liberty, freedom of association and freedom of expression."[58] Human Rights Watch (HRW) found that Venezuelan security forces repeatedly resorted to force, including lethal force, against peaceful, unarmed protesters and bystanders "in situations in which it was wholly unjustified."[59] HRW noted that these abuses included "severely beating unarmed individuals; firing live ammunition, rubber bullets, and teargas canisters indiscriminately into crowds; and firing rubber bullets deliberately, at point-blank range, at unarmed individuals."[60] Amnesty International (AI) corroborated these accounts and noted that, contrary to international standards, state security forces used firearms against protesters without providing adequate warning.[61] AI also reported on the "excessive and indiscriminate" use of tear gas by police.[62]

In its December 2014 review of Venezuela, the U.N. Committee Against Torture noted "with concern that 43 people died in the context of the demonstrations that occurred between February and June 2014, and 878 were wounded, of which 68 percent were civilians,"[63] noting consistent reports regarding the excessive use of force. The Committee also expressed concern regarding the abuse of firearms and riot control agents against demonstrators and in residential areas, as well as the involvement of the National Guard in controlling demonstrations as opposed to civilian police forces.[64]

The Committee Against Torture also reported a total of 437 attacks by armed pro-government groups against protesters during demonstrations between February and April 2014, noting that a large number of these attacks were carried out with the complicity and acquiescence of the state security forces, and went unpunished.[65] Human Rights Watch also noted that armed pro-government groups attacked protesters, journalists, and persons perceived to be opposed to the government in the presence of security forces and with impunity. In some cases, state security forces openly collaborated with pro-government groups in committing these attacks.[66] The Inter-American Commission on Human Rights condemned attacks of this nature and noted that they occurred in many parts of the country.[67]

Protests have reignited since February of this year after the arrest of the Caracas Metropolitan Mayor Antonio Ledezma. Violent repression and the use of military force during these demonstrations have already resulted in new fatal victims, wounded persons and arbitrary arrests. On February 24, Kluiverth Roa Nunez, a 14-year-old high school student was killed by a gunshot wound in the head during the clashes between students of the Catholic University of Tachira (UCAT) and security forces. Reports indicate that the boy was not even participating in the protests.[68]

III. Lack of judicial independence

In May 2004 the National Assembly passed a new Organic Law of the Supreme Court, which completely weakened Venezuela's judicial branch.[69] This Organic Law increased the membership of the Supreme Court from 20 to 32 justices and established that the new Justices could be designated with a simple majority vote of the National Assembly, making it easier for the Government and its majority in the legislative to take control of the country's highest Court. Since this political takeover of the Supreme Court of Justice, its members have publicly rejected the principle of separation of powers and the judiciary has acted as another arm of the executive branch to advance the government's political agenda by legitimizing its policies and decisions, consistently ruling in its favor and "validating the government's disregard for human rights."[70]

But the weakness of the judiciary precedes 2004 and is also a consequence of the inadequate transition in the Judicial branch following the adoption of the 1999 Constitution, which has resulted in the practice of appointing provisional or interim judges. For over a decade, the Judicial Commission of the Supreme Court has been discretionally ordering the removal of hundreds of provisional judges without a prior disciplinary proceeding, denying Venezuelan's judges one of the most basic safeguards for their independence: security of tenure.

It is estimated that 62 per cent of the judges in Venezuela are provisional, and therefore can be easily appointed and removed.[71] As underscored by the IACHR, the high number of provisional appointments "weakens the judicial branch and strips it of its independence and impartiality, thereby adversely affecting the right of access to justice."[72] The Special Rapporteur on the independence of judges and lawyers has also expressed his concern over the high number of judges and prosecutors who are provisional, considering that they are "subject to various mechanisms of political interference that affect their independence," in particular bearing in mind that their removal is "absolutely discretional: without cause, or procedure, or an effective judicial remedy."[73]

One of the most notorious examples of interference by the Executive in the administration of justice has been the case of *Maria Lourdes Afiuni*. A judge at the 31st control Court of Caracas, in December 2009 Afiuni granted conditional release to a businessman critic of the government who had been awaiting trial on corruption charges for almost 3 years. She was immediately arrested and President Chavez called Judge Afiuni a "bandit", asking for her to be given a 30-year prison sentence despite her compliance with U.N. standards and Venezuelan law. Afiuni was formally accused of corruption, abuse of authority, and favoring evasion of justice.[74] After over a year in a women's prison in Caracas under deplorable conditions and where she repeatedly suffered to threats and acts of intimidation by other inmates,[75] she was put under house arrest in February 2011. On June 14, 2013, the judicial authorities lifted the house arrest but her trial continues.[76]

The case of Judge Afiuni has captured the international attention and generated calls from U.N. experts and the inter-American System of human rights urging for her "immediate and unconditional release."[77] However, as denounced by Human Rights Watch in a comprehensive report on this issue, the arrest of Judge Afiuni has had a powerful impact on lower court judges who have been afraid to issue rulings that may upset the government, and "whereas in the past they only feared losing their jobs, now they also fear being criminally prosecuted for upholding the law."[78]

As recently as last month, Ali Fabricio Paredes, another judge—who incidentally presided over Afiuni's case at some point—was arrested by national intelligence agents, less than 24 hours after he had convicted Walid Makled to 14 years in prison for drug-trafficking and money-laundering. The Attorney General ordered Judge Paredes' arrest for considering that he had unduly favored Makled with a lenient prison sentence.[79]

IV. Arbitrary arrests and detentions

The Venezuelan Constitution prohibits the arrest or detention of an individual without a judicial order and provides that any detained individual has the right to immediately communicate with family and lawyers. But in practice, it is estimated that more than 70 people have been arbitrarily detained or arrested in Venezuela over the last year alone.[80]

The use of arbitrary arrest and detention in Venezuela is not recent. However, international human rights organizations have registered an increase in the number of people arbitrarily detained since 2014, particularly around the protests against the Government. According to official information, 3,306 people were arrested, including 400 adolescents, between February and June of 2014 in the context of the public protests that took place across the country.[81] It was reported that of the thousands of people arrested many were denied access to a lawyer of their choice and to medical assistance during the first 48 hours of their detention before appearing before a judge. Some of the people arrested remained in pre-trial detention for several months, in spite of the absence of solid evidence against them.[82] Even the U.N. High Commissioner for Human Rights expressed concern over the prolonged and arbitrary detention of political opponents and protestors in Venezuela, and stated that it was only " exacerbating the tensions in the country."[83]

Notably, one of the individuals that were arrested in connection to the February 2014 protests is Leopoldo Lopez, leader of the opposition party Voluntad Popular. After been accused of promoting violence in the antigovernment demonstrations that started a few days later, on 18 February 2014 Leopoldo Lopez handed himself in to the National Guard. He has remained in pre-trial detention since, with charges of incitement and conspiracy to commit arson and damages to property, among other offences, which could carry a maximum penalty of 10 years of prison.[84]

A month after Leopoldo Lopez' detention, members of the Intelligence Security Services (SEBIN) arrested Daniel Ceballos, mayor of San Cristobal (Tachira State) and also a member of opposition party Voluntad Popular on suspicion of rebellion and conspiracy to commit a crime for his involvement in the antigovernment protests that had taken place in February. No arrest warrant was produced at the time of his arrest and shortly after, the Minister of Justice and Interior of Venezuela posted several messages on Twitter claiming that justice had been done and accusing Ceballos of promoting violence, anarchy, and civil rebellion.[85]

In August 2014, the United Nations Working Group on Arbitrary Detentions adopted an opinion concerning Leopoldo Lopez, concluding that his detention was arbitrary. It considered that "Mr. Lopez's participation in a march for political reasons or the exercising of his right to freedom of expression during the same march, such as which took place on February 12, 2014, does not constitute an illicit justification for the deprivation of liberty of a speaker or participant." It further stated that in his case "there are no elements that allow the concluding of a cause-and-effect relationship between the call for a political demonstration, speaking during the same demonstration, and the resulting deaths, wounds, and material damage."[86] The Working Group also found that "the detention of Mr. Lopez in a military compound seems based on a motive of discrimination based on his political opinions."[87] The Working Group also found the detention of Daniel Ceballos to be arbitrary.[88]

The U.N. High Commissioner for Human Rights, also expressed serious concern at the continued detention of Venezuelan opposition leader Leopoldo Lopez, as well as more than 69 other people who were arrested in the context of the public protests that started in February 2014. He further called on the Venezuelan authorities "to act on the opinions of the Working Group and immediately release Mr Lopez and Mr Ceballos, as well as all those detained for exercising their legitimate right to express themselves and protest peacefully."[89] Both Lopez and Ceballos remain in detention to date, despite repeated calls from the international community for their immediate release.

Exactly 1 year after Leopoldo Lopez's arrest, on February 19, 2015, Caracas Metropolitan mayor, Antonio Ledezma, was arrested and thereby expelled from office. Mr. Ledezma is an opposition leader and ally of Leopoldo Lopez. According to Mr. Ledezma's wife, intelligence agents forcibly entered his office and beat the mayor before dragging him away. Soon afterward, President Nicolas Maduro publicly denounced Mr. Ledezma as a "vampire" and accused him of conspiring with the United States and other foreign governments to foment a coup.[90] President Maduro said he would respond "with an iron fist."[91] The evidence presented of this alleged conspiracy is a statement that Mr. Ledezma signed along with other opposition leaders published in a national newspaper, which highlighted the multiple challenges facing the country and called for an agreement to reach a peaceful and democratic transition. As such, his arrest was clearly politically motivated and arbitrary.

V. Torture and cruel, inhumane, and degrading treatment in prisons

Political prisoners in Venezuela have been subject to torture and other cruel, inhuman, and degrading treatment while in custody. The scale of these human rights violations seems to have increased since antigovernment protests began last year, but follows a long-standing pattern. Reports to this end have been issued from multiple international and regional organizations including the Inter-American Commission on Human Rights; the Office of the High Commissioner for Human Rights; and the United Nations Committee Against Torture; as well as countless nongovernmental organizations such as Human Rights Watch and Amnesty International.

The U.N. Committee Against Torture expressed alarm regarding reported acts of torture and ill-treatment of persons arrested in connection with the demonstrations which occurred in Venezuela between February and June 2014. These acts include beatings, electric shocks, burns, suffocation, sexual violence and threats, apparently to punish protesters and obtain confessions.[92] Similarly, in most cases documented by Human Rights Watch in its report regarding last year's protests, security forces subjected those arrested for protesting to severe physical abuse, including beatings with fists, helmets, and firearms; being forced to squat or kneel, without moving, for hours at a time; and extended exposure to extreme temperatures.[93] Human Rights Watch also reported cases of torture including a pattern of firing rubber bullets point blank at protesters, withholding medical treatment despite life-threatening injuries, and psychological abuse.[94] Amnesty International reported similar horrific accounts of abuse against detainees in its report and highlighted that inhuman and degrading treatment of detainees appeared to be in retaliation for their involvement in protests. For example, both male and female detainees reported being raped or threatened with rape by security agents. Other reports of torture and inhuman and degrading treatment include detainees being repeatedly and intentionally run over or hit by police officers on motorcycles; being doused in gasoline; and being subjected to severe beatings with batons.[95]

Inhumane treatment of detainees continues to this day. Last week, Rodolfo Gonzalez, a political prisoner and former aviation pilot, committed suicide in prison. He was reportedly suffering from extreme physical and emotional distress due to the conditions of his detention at the headquarters of the State Intelligence Service

(SEBIN) and the news that he would soon be transferred to an extremely dangerous prison known as "Yare." [96]

In the heart of Caracas is a prison known as "La Tumba" ("the tomb"). Located five stories below ground are holding cells for protesters and political prisoners. Prisoners of La Tumba are not only confined to tight spaces and constantly exposed to subfreezing temperatures, but are also deprived of sunlight, sanitary conditions, and ventilation. The conditions of detention have reportedly caused all inmates to become extremely ill, with symptoms including severe vomiting, diarrhea, fever, and hallucinations. However, they are denied access to adequate medical treatment. [97]

Just earlier this month, the IACHR granted precautionary measures for the protection of political prisoners, Lorent Saleh and Gerardo Carrero. [98] These measures, which are only granted in extreme cases of urgency, gravity, and threats of irreparable harm, were issued based on reliable reports that the detention conditions of Mr. Saleh and Mr. Carrero put their lives and safety at risk. These deplorable conditions have resulted in injuries and illness, for which no adequate medical treatment is provided. In issuing the precautionary measures, the IACHR referred to multiple reports it had investigated and received in recent years regarding serious violations of the human rights of detainees in Venezuela. [99]

The inhumane conditions in Venezuelan prisons are not only suffered by political prisoners are exacerbated by extreme overcrowding. During the first half of 2014, jails were reported to be at 190 percent capacity. [100] Additionally, as noted by the Committee Against Torture, detainees were deprived of medical care, potable water, food, sanitation, and ventilation. [101] Further, 309 prisoners died in Venezuelan prisons during 2014 alone, [102] but the numbers of inmates that have died in prison since 2004 is 4,791 and 9,931 have been wounded in the last decade. [103]

The CAT Committee highlighted reports that political prisoners such as Leopoldo Lopez, have been held in solitary confinement. [104] There have been numerous reports regarding the cruel, inhuman, and degrading treatment of Mr. Lopez, who is detained in Ramo Verde prison. For example, in October guards ordered Mr. Lopez and other detainees to defecate into plastic bags, and subsequently threw the same bags of human excrement at them and prevented them from bathing. [105]

Last February 13, Mr. Lopez's cell was forcibly broken into for the apparent purpose of attacking and intimidating him. Since then, Mr. Lopez has been held in isolation, and deprived of communication with his lawyers and family, in direct violation of his rights. [106] The U.N. Special Rapporteur on Torture recently expressed that Venezuela had violated international law "by failing to take measures to prevent mistreatment" and "torture" of demonstrators and detainees, including the imposition of solitary confinement to opposition leader Leopoldo Lopez and the recent violent searches in the cells of other political prisoners such as Daniel Ceballos, Enzo Scarano, and Salvatore Luchesse. [107]

VI. Violations of the right to political participation

The right to participate in one's political system is a fundamental right, which not only gives citizens a voice in their own government, but also protects human rights defenders, supports underrepresented and vulnerable populations, and prevents violent political transitions. [108] The rights to vote, participate in, and benefit from public service are protected by international instruments such as the Universal Declaration of Human Rights (UDHR) [109] and the International Covenant on Civil and Political Rights (ICCPR). [110] Article 21 of the UDHR provides that "Everyone has the right to take part in the government of his country, directly or through freely chosen representatives." ICCPR article 25 affirms that "Every citizen shall have the right and the opportunity . . . (a) To take part in the conduct of public affairs, directly or through freely chosen representatives; (b) To vote and to be elected at genuine periodic elections . . . (c) To have access, on general terms of equality, to public service in his country." Likewise, the American Declaration on the Rights and Duties of Man [111] states in Article XX: "Every person having legal capacity is entitled to participate in the government of his country, directly or through his representatives, and to take part in popular elections, which shall be by secret ballot, and shall be honest, periodic, and free."

Despite these legal obligations enshrined in international law and freely accepted by the state of Venezuela, the government has repeatedly stymied the right to political participation for opposition leaders, thereby repressing the rights of individuals as well as limiting free discourse and debate about matters in the public interest. Specifically, opposition leaders have both been denied the right to run for office and arbitrarily expelled from their positions.

Leopoldo Lopez, leader of the opposition party Voluntad Popular (Popular Will), was elected mayor of the Chacao municipality of Caracas in July 2000. Mr. Lopez was recognized for his commitment to transparency and accountability. [112] However, in August and September 2005 the government imposed sanctions for alleged corruption which had the effect of disqualifying Mr. Lopez from public office for a period of 3 and 6 years, respectively.[113] Mr. Lopez was thus prevented from running for mayor in 2008. In 2011, the Inter-American Court of Human Rights issued a unanimous decision on this matter in favor of Mr. Lopez.[114] The Inter-American Court found that the alleged charges of corruption brought against Mr. Lopez, which he maintained were baseless, were never adjudicated by a competent tribunal and that Mr. Lopez was never charged with a crime. The Inter-American Court held that Mr. Lopez's human right to political participation had been violated. However, the Venezuelan regime refused to abide by the ruling, and Mr. Lopez was thus prevented from running in the 2012 Presidential election.[115] As described above, Leopoldo Lopez has been arbitrarily detained since February 18, 2014, in the military prison of Ramo Verde, specifically for exercising his rights to political participation and other human rights.

Multiple elected officials who are opposition party members have been arbitrary expelled or threatened with expulsion from their positions. For example, Maria Corina Machado, an opposition leader and the founder, former vice president, and former president of the Venezuelan volunteer civil organization Sumate, was stripped of her seat in the National Assembly after being accused of treason by President Maduro in 2014. She had previously been charged with conspiracy for funds Sumate received from the National Endowment for Democracy (NED).[116]

Ms. Machado ran for the National Assembly in 2010 and received the highest number of votes in the country.[117] Ms. Machado has been one of the most vocal critics of President Maduro and the late President Chavez. She has repeatedly called for the removal of Mr. Maduro by legal means. In March 2014, after she accepted Panama's invitation to speak about repression in Venezuela at the Organization of American States General Assembly, and in response to her vocal support of the antigovernment protests last year, she was expelled from the National Assembly.[118] By arbitrarily ousting Ms. Machado, the government violated her right to political participation and inhibited free expression and dissent among the legislature. The Inter-American Commission on Human Rights expressed concern about the reported "lack of guarantees to ensure due process in the investigations and prosecutions" of Ms. Machado and other members of the opposition.[119]

Further evidence of the government's campaign to silence dissent and violate the right to political participation came last month, when the ruling party in the National Assembly moved to strip opposition party Congressman Julio Borges of his seat.[120] Legislators called for an investigation into Mr. Borges, accusing him of conspiring along with Mr. Ledezma to foment a coup to overthrow President Maduro. The National Assembly President, Diosdado Cabello, also accused him of planning to murder Leopoldo Lopez to create chaos.[121] Like other opposition leaders accused of plotting to overthrow the government, Mr. Borges would lose his legislative immunity if expelled from Congress, and thus could be prosecuted.[122] The pattern of repression of the right to political participation thus has a chilling effect on all Venezuelans who hold dissenting views and wish to advocate for democratic change.

Mr. Chairman, Ranking Member Boxer, and members of the Subcommittee on the Western Hemisphere, the disregard by the Venezuelan Government of the human rights of its people is absolute. The account I have just presented is only but a fraction of the grave and systematic violations that are taking place in that country but show the speedy deterioration of the security and enjoyment of the most basic rights and freedoms of the Venezuelan people. It is time for the international community to ensure through multilateral and bilateral efforts that democracy and the rule of law are respected in Venezuela. In 2001, the hemisphere adopted the Democratic Charter to address challenges such as the ones Venezuela is going through. The U.S. Government should work together with the Organization of American States (OAS), the Union of South American Nations (UNASUR) and the leaders of the region to ensure that the Democratic Charter is respected.

End Notes

[1] According to the information published by the Office of the High Commissioner for Human Rights (OHCHR), only a visit by the Special Rapporteur on the Right to Food was accepted by the Government of Venezuela in 2011 but it has not yet taken place.

[2] HRW, "Venezuela: Human Rights Watch Delegation Expelled," September 19, 2008.

[3] Committee Against Torture (CAT), Concluding Observations: Bolivarian Republic of Venezuela, UN Doc. CAT/C/VEN/CO/3–4 (in Spanish), December 12, 2014, para. 8.

[4] Law authorizing the President of the Republic to Issue Decrees with the Level, Strength and Validity of Laws on delegated matters. Articles 1 and 2. Published in Extraordinary Official Gazette No. 6.112 of November 19, 2013.

50

[5] Reuters, "Venezuela's Maduro seeks decree powers to face U.S. 'imperialism'", March 10, 2015.

[6] Resolution No. 008610 of the Ministry of Defense published in the Official Gazette on January 27, 2015.

[7] CAT, Concluding Observations: Bolivarian Republic of Venezuela, para. 15.

[8] The Petrocaribe program established in 2005 by Venezuela is described as a development cooperation program through energy supply assistance. Official page of Petrocaribe: http://www.petrocaribe.org/.

[9] FAO, Progress is proof that hunger can be eliminated, press release of June 16 2013.

[10] IACHR, Annual Report 2013, para. 667.

[11] Aporrea.org, "Venezuela pide a la FAO apoyo para sistema de oferta de alimentos," June 16, 2013, as cited in IACHR, Annual Report 2013, para. 669.

[12] Decree No. 8,331 with rank, value and force of Law on Costs and Fair Prices. Published in Official Gazette No. 39,715, of July 18, 2011.

[13] CNN, "Facing shortages, Venezuela takes over toilet paper factory," September 21, 2013.

[14] Bloomberg, "Venezuelans Throng Grocery Stores Under Military Protection," January 9 2015.

[15] U.N., "Venezuela: U.N. Human Rights Chief Urges Halt to Violence, Inflammatory Rhetoric," Feb. 28, 2014.

[16] Freedom House." Venezuela: Freedom of the Press 2014."

[17] Id.

[18] HRW, "Venezuela: Legislative Assault on Free Speech, Civil Society," Dec. 22, 2010.

[19] Freedom House, "Venezuelan Government Silencing Media During Protests, Undermining Free Expression," Feb. 21, 2014.

[20] El Nacional, "300 desempleados ha dejado cierre de periódicos," Feb. 8, 2014.

[21] Freedom House, "Venezuelan Government Silencing Media During Protests, Undermining Free Expression," Feb. 21, 2014.

[22] IACHR "Annual Report of the Office of the Special Rapporteur for Freedom of Expression: 2013," OEA/Ser.L/V/II.149 Doc. 50 Dec. 31, 2013.

[23] IACHR, "IACHR Expresses Deep Concern over Acts of Violence in Venezuela and Urges the State to Ensure Democratic Citizen Security," press release No. 13 of Feb. 14, 2014.

[24] Id.

[25] Freedom House, "Freedom of the Press 2003: Venezuela."

[26] Id.

[27] Id.

[28] HRW, "World Report 2014: Venezuela."

[29] Reporters without Borders, "Venezuela."

[30] Reporters without Borders, "World Press Freedom Index 2014: Venezuela."

[31] Reporters without Borders, "Venezuela."

[32] Committee to Protect Journalists (CPJ), "In Venezuela, Campaign to Silence Press."

[33] Id.

[34] CAT, Concluding Observations: Bolivarian Republic of Venezuela, December 12, 2014, para. 14.

[35] Freedom House, "Venezuelan Government Silencing Media During Protests, Undermining Free Expression," Feb. 21, 2014.

[36] IACHR., "Annual Report of the Office of the Special Rapporteur for Freedom of Expression: 2013," OEA/Ser.L/V/II.149, Doc. 50, Dec. 31, 2013.

[37] Id.

[38] IACHR, "Office of the Special Rapporteur Expresses Concern over the Situation of the Freedom of Expression in Venezuela," Sept. 22, 2014.

[39] IACtHR., "Case of Perozo et al. v. Venezuela", Series C No. 195, January 28, 2009.

[40] HRW, "Venezuela: Unarmed Protestors Beaten, Shot," May 5, 2014.

[41] Resolution No. 008610 of the Ministry of Defense published in the Official Gazette on January 27, 2015.

[42] HRW, "Venezuela: Legislative Assault on Free Speech, Civil Society," Dec. 22, 2010.

[43] Id.

[44] Id.

[45] Id.

[46] Int'l. Ctr. for Not-for-Profit Law, "NGO Law Monitor: Venezuela," Dec. 1, 2014.

[47] See, e.g. Vision Global, "Capriles: "Cespa busca ocultar realidad de los venezolanos," 2013. Available (in Spanish). Manzana Mecanica, "Venezuela censura Twitter y fortalece CESPA: duro golpe a la libertad de información," Feb. 28, 2014.

[48] IACHR, "Annual Report 2009: Chapter IV, Human Rights Developments in the Region: Venezuela," OEA/Ser.L/V/II. Doc. 51, corr. 1, Dec. 30, 2009.

[49] Id.

[50] Id.

[51] Freedom House, "Venezuela: Freedom in the World 2013." See also PROVEA, "Provea rechaza la criminalización de la protesta y dvierte sobre la institucionalización de la mentalidad represiva en la acción de gobierno," Feb. 7, 2014.

[52] Freedom House, "Freedom of Association Under Threat: The New Authoritarians' Offensive Against Civil Society."

[53] See International Covenant on Civil and Political Rights [hereinafter ICCPR] art. 21, art. 22(2), 999 U.N.T.S. 171, entered into force Mar. 23, 1976; Manfred Nowak, U.N. Covenant on Civil and Political Rights: CCPR Commentary 487–488 (2005). See generally Basic Principles on the Use of Force and Firearms by Law Enforcement Officials (1990), available at http://www2.ohchr.org/english/law/firearms.htm [hereinafter "Use of force principles"].

[54] Code of Conduct for Law Enforcement Officials art. 3, G.A. Res. 34/169 (1979).

[55] Code of Conduct, art. 3.

[56] Use of force principles, at 5.

[57] Use of force principles, at 5.

[58] IACHR, ''IACHR expresses deep concern over the situation with respect to the right to peaceful protest, freedom of association and freedom of expression in Venezuela,'' press release No. 17 of February 21, 2014.

[59] HRW, ''World Report 2012: Venezuela,'' p. 9.

[60] Id. at p. 8.

[61] Amnesty International, ''Venezuela: Human rights at risk amid protests'' (AMR 53/009/2014), April 1, 2014, p. 5.

[62] Id. at p. 6.

[63] CAT, Concluding Observations: Bolivarian Republic of Venezuela, December 12, 2014, para. 12.

[64] Id.

[65] Id. at para. 13.

[66] HRW, ''World Report 2012: Venezuela,'' p.12.

[67] IACHR, ''IACHR expresses deep concern over the situation with respect to the right to peaceful protest, freedom of association and freedom of expression in Venezuela,'' press release No. 17 of February 21, 2014.

[68] IACHR, ''IACHR Laments the Death of a Student during Protests in Venezuela,'' press release no. 22 of March 3, 2015. See also Amnesty international, public declaration of February 25, 2015 (in Spanish).

[69] ''Ley Orgánica del Tribunal Supremo de Justicia (2004).

[70] HRW, Submission to the Human Rights Committee in advance to its presessional review of Venezuela, July 29 2014.

[71] CAT, Concluding Observations: Bolivarian Republic of Venezuela, December 12, 2014, para. 16.

[72] IACHR, Annual Report 2013, para. 441.

[73] OHCHR, ''Preocupante la situación de la justicia en Venezuela, advierte experto de la ONU,'' July 30, 2009.

[74] HRW, ''Tightening the Grip: Concentration and Abuse of Power in Chávez's Venezuela,'' July 2012, pp. 30–36.

[75] ID at p. 36.

[76] BBC, ''Venezuela ends house arrest of Judge Maria Afiuni,'' June 14, 2013.

[77] U.N. News Centre, ''Venezuelan leader violates independence of judiciary—U.N. rights experts,'' 16 December 2009.

[78] HRW, ''Tightening the Grip: Concentration and Abuse of Power in Chávez's Venezuela,'' July 2012, p. 5. See also IACHR, Annual Report 2013, para. 660.

[79] International Bar Association, ''IBAHRI expresses grave concern at arrests and further deterioration of rule of law in Venezuela,'' 18 February 2015.

[80] OHCHR, U.N. Human Rights Chief urges Venezuela to release arbitrarily detained protestors and politicians, 20 October 2014.

[81] CAT, Concluding Observations: Bolivarian Republic of Venezuela, December 12, 2014, para. 9.

[82] CAT, Concluding Observations: Bolivarian Republic of Venezuela, December 12, 2014, para. 9. See also Amnesty International, Report 2014/15, Venezuela.

[83] OHCHR, U.N. Human Rights Chief urges Venezuela to release arbitrarily detained protestors and politicians, 20 October 2014.

[84] Amnesty International, Venezuela: Trial of opposition leader Leopoldo Lopez raises concerns about the independence of the justice system in Venezuela, 21 July 2014.

[85] Amnesty International, Venezuela: Arrest of local mayor signals potential ''witch hunt,'' 20 March 2014.

[86] Opinion Number 26/2014 (Bolivarian Republic of Venezuela) adopted by the Working Group on Arbitrary Detention at its seventieth session, August 25–29, 2014, para. 54.

[87] Id. at para. 55.

[88] OHCHR, U.N. Human Rights Chief urges Venezuela to release arbitrarily detained protestors and politicians, 20 October 2014.

[89] OHCHR, U.N. Human Rights Chief urges Venezuela to release arbitrarily detained protestors and politicians, 20 October 2014.

[90] El Pais, ''La policía de Maduro detiene al alcalde opositor de Caracas,'' February 20, 2015. Available (In Spanish).

[91] Id.

[92] CAT, Concluding Observations: Bolivarian Republic of Venezuela, December 12, 2014, para. 10. See also U.N. Human Rights Chief urges Venezuela to release arbitrarily detained protestors and politicians, October 20, 2014.

[93] Human Rights Watch, ''Punished for Protesting: Rights Violations in Venezuela's Streets, Detention Centers, and Justice System'' 2014, pp. 15.

[94] Id. at p. 17

[95] Amnesty International, ''Venezuela: Human rights at risk amid protests'' (AMR 53/009/2014), April 1, 2014.

[96] ''Muere en prisión Rodolfo González, opositor detenido en manifestaciones en Venezuela,'' BBC Mundo, March 13, 2015. Available (in Spanish).

[97] ABC.es, '' 'La tumba,' siete celdas de tortura en el corazón de Caracas,'' February 10, 2015.

[98] IACHR, Resolution 6/2015, Precautionary Measure No 223–13, ''Matter of Lorent Saleh y Gerardo Carrero regarding Venezuela,'' March 2, 2015.

[99] Id. at para. 16.

[100] CAT, Concluding Observations: Bolivarian Republic of Venezuela, December 12, 2014, para. 18.

[101] See generally CAT, Concluding Observations: Bolivarian Republic of Venezuela, December 12, 2014.

[102] Venezuelan Prisons Observatory. See more information (in Spanish) at: http://elimpulso.com/articulo/violencia-en-carceles-venezolanas-dejo-309-reclusos-muertos-en-2014.

[103] CAT, Concluding Observations: Bolivarian Republic of Venezuela, December 12, 2014, para. 19.

[104] Id. at para. 18.

[105] Juan Carlos Vargas, "Caso Leopoldo López: Situación actual del juicio, violaciones de DDHH y pronunciamientos internacionales," Acción por la Libertad, January 30, 2015 (in Spanish, on file with author).

[106] Americas Quarterly, "Meeting with Vice President Biden Triggers Alleged Retaliation from Venezuelan Government," February 13, 2015.

[107] El Heraldo, "Venezuela no previno actos de torturas," relator de ONU, March 12, 2015. Available (in Spanish) at:http://www.elheraldo.co/internacional/venezuela-no-previno-actos-de-torturas-relator-de-onu-187298.

[108] See "Political Participation: A Fundamental Right in Need of Protection," submission by Human Rights Advocates and University of San Francisco School of Law's International Human Rights Clinic to the U.N. Human Rights Council.

[109] U.N. General Assembly, Universal Declaration of Human Rights, 10 December 1948, 217 A (III).

[110] ICCPR. Ratified by Venezuela on May 10, 1978. Ratified by the United States of America on June 8, 1992.

[111] American Declaration of the Rights and Duties of Man, O.A.S. Res. XXX, adopted by the Ninth International Conference of American States (1948)

[112] See, e.g. "Premio Transparencia 2008 para Leopoldo López," October 6, 2008.

[113] IACtHR, "Case of López Mendoza v. Venezuela," Judgment of September 1, 2011 (Merits, Reparations, and Costs), Series C No. 233.

[114] Id.

[115] See, e.g., Jeremy McDermott, "Chavez accused of behaving like 'dictator' ahead of elections," The Telegraph (UK), November 21, 2008.

[116] HRW, "Venezuela: Court Orders Trial of Civil Society Leaders," July 8, 2005.

[117] Mery Mogollon and Chris Kraul, "Venezuela elections weaken Chavez's hold," Los Angeles Times, September 28, 2010.

[118] "Venezuela opposition congresswoman's mandate revoked," BBC News, March 24 2014.

[119] IACHR, "IACHR Expresses Deep Concern over the Situation regarding the Rule of Law in Venezuela," press release No. 15 of February 24, 2015.

[120] Sara Schaefer Munoz and Ezequiel Minaya, "Venezuela Cracks Down on Dissent," Wall Street Journal, February 24, 2015.

[121] The Star, "Venezuela's Ruling Socialists Target Another Opposition Leader," February 24, 2015.

[122] The New York Times, "Clashes, Tear Gas After Police Kill Boy at Venezuela Protest", February 25, 2015.

Senator RUBIO. Thank you.

Mr. Farah.

STATEMENT OF DOUGLAS FARAH, PRESIDENT, IBI CONSULTANTS, TAKOMA PARK, MD

Mr. FARAH. Thank you, Chairman Rubio, for the chance to be here today to discuss the accelerating crisis in Venezuela and its implications for the United States and regional security. I speak only on behalf of myself, and my views are not necessarily those of CSIS or IASC.

I want to focus on Venezuela's regional role rather than its internal problems because I believe this is where the strategic threat to the United States actually resides.

There is little doubt that Venezuela has, for a decade now, posed a significant threat not only to U.S. security interests in the Western Hemisphere but to the survival of democracy and the rule of law in the region. A recent investigation by Veja, a respected Brazilian magazine, shows that Venezuela, with the help of Argentina, actively tried to help Iran's nuclear program in violation of international sanctions. More than a dozen Venezuelan officials have been publicly identified by U.S. law enforcement as being directly involved in drug trafficking or the support of terrorist groups.

The threat originating in Venezuela is not confined to Venezuela. The late Hugo Chavez, acting in concert with his allies, Rafael

Correa in Ecuador, Evo Morales in Bolivia, Daniel Ortega in Nicaragua, and Cristina Fernandez de Kirchner in Argentina, set out to redefine the political landscape in Latin America. And to a large degree, they have been successful. Unfortunately, the changes wrought under the banner of ''Socialism for the 21st Century'' have brought massive corruption, rising violence, and repression. Venezuela is the indisputable leader and primary axis around which the others revolve.

Venezuela and its allies have moved perilously close to becoming criminalized states, that is, states where the senior leadership is involved with, and act in concert with, transnational organized crime groups as a matter of statecraft. The Maduro administration is the central component of a multistate, ongoing criminal enterprise, carried out in concert with Iran and a growing Russian presence, whose primary strategic objective is to cling to power by whatever means necessary and harm the United States and its allies. In this endeavor, it has embraced the FARC, Hezbollah, ETA of Spain, the Sinaloa Cartel, and other terrorist and drug trafficking organizations and—I repeat—as a matter of state policy, not as rogue elements acting on their own.

The stakes in the unfolding crisis in Venezuela for United States interests and the survival of democracy in Latin America are high. The consequences of the growth of this poisonous Bolivarian criminal enterprise is lethal.

Few understood this better than Alberto Nisman, the courageous Argentine prosecutor who was investigating the 1994 Iran-backed bombing of the AMIA Jewish Center in Buenos Aires. Before being murdered on January 18, Nisman had documented the Bolivarian-Iran ties across the Western Hemisphere, including two attempted attacks backed by Iran in the United States. Iran, identified by successive U.S. administrations as a state sponsor of terror, has expanded its political alliances, diplomatic presence, trade initiatives, military and intelligence programs in the Bolivarian axis primarily through its deep ties with Venezuela.

The Iranian Constitution, first pointed out by Prosecutor Nisman, is an extraordinary document in which Iran stakes its claim to world domination in the name of Allah. The preamble to the Iranian Constitution states: ''With due consideration for the Islamic Element of the Iranian Revolution, which has been a movement for the victory of all oppressed peoples who are confronted with aggressors, this Constitution shall pave the way for the perpetuation of this revolution within and outside the country. This Constitution seeks to lay the groundwork for the creation of a single world nation and perpetuate the struggle to make this nation a reality for all the world's needy and oppressed nations.'' That is quite a statement for a constitution.

This is the country with whom Venezuela and the Bolivarian states have chosen to align themselves while seeking to eradicate U.S. influence. U.S. influence is being replaced by a lethal doctrine of asymmetrical warfare inspired by an authoritarian government seeking perpetual power and nurtured by Iran in its overt desire to violently spread its brand of Islamic revolution.

In addition to serving as a gateway for Iran's presence in the region, Venezuela has also been the primary conduit for Russia's growing presence in the region, something that is of growing concern in our national security community. And I deal with this at length in my written statement.

In my written testimony, I detail many of the other cases to substantiate the statements that I make here.

But I want to close with the words of the legendary Manhattan district attorney, Robert Morgenthau, as he retired in 2009 after decades of public service, including the pursuit of numerous and ongoing criminal investigations into the Venezuelan Government's criminal activities. He said: "Let there be no doubt that Hugo Chavez leads not only a corrupt government but one staffed with terrorist sympathizers. The government has strong ties to narcotrafficking and money laundering, and reportedly plays an active role in the transshipment of narcotics and the laundering of narcotics proceeds in exchange for payments to corrupt government officials." Under the even less competent hands of Nicolas Maduro, the situation described by Morgenthau 6 years ago has grown considerably worse, as has the threat.

Thank you very much.

[The prepared statement of Mr. Farah follows:]

PREPARED STATEMENT OF DOUGLAS FARAH

Chairman Rubio, Ranking Member Boxer and members of the committee, thank you for the invitation today to discuss the ongoing and accelerating crisis in Venezuela and its implications for the United States and regional security issues. I speak on behalf of only IBI Consultants and myself. The views are mine and do not necessarily reflect those of CSIS or IASC.

There is little doubt that Venezuela has for a decade now posed a significant threat not only to U.S. security interests in the Western Hemisphere, but to the survival of democracy and the rule of law in the region. A recent investigation by Veja, a respected Brazilian magazine, shows that Venezuela, with the help of Argentina, actively tried to help Iran's nuclear program in violation of international sanctions.[1] More than a dozen senior Venezuelan officials have been publicly identified by U.S. officials as being directly involved in supporting and participating in drug trafficking and support of designated terrorist groups.

The threat originating in Venezuela is not confined to Venezuela. The late Hugo Chavez, acting in concert with his allies Rafael Correa in Ecuador, Evo Morales in Bolivia, Daniel Ortega in Nicaragua, Cristina Fernandez de Kirchner in Argentina, set out to redefine the political landscape in Latin America. And to a large degree they have been successful. Unfortunately the changes wrought under the banner of "Socialism for the 21st Century" have brought massive corruption; rising violence; a disdain for the rule of law; the rise of equating an individual leader as the state ("Chavez is Venezuela"); a significant and ongoing, concerted effort to silence peaceful opposition and independent media; and collapse of institutions designed to guarantee oversight and transparency of public individuals and entities.

My testimony will focus on this alliance, of which Venezuela is the indisputable leader and primary axis around which the others revolve. However, and this is what presents the greater strategic threat emanating from Venezuela, it is not acting alone, but in concert with multiple other nations.

Venezuela and its allies have moved perilously close to being "criminalized states," that is, states where the senior leadership is aware of and involved and act on behalf of the state, with transnational organized crime (TOC), where TOC is used as an instrument of statecraft, and where levers of state power are incorporated into the operational structure of one or more TOC groups.[2] The Maduro administration is the central component to a multistate ongoing criminal enterprise, carried out in concert with Iran and a growing Russian presence, whose primary strategic objective is to cling to power by whatever means necessary and harm the United States and its allies.

Democracy was far from perfect before the advent of the "Bolivarian Revolution," as Chavez defined his movement. Many of the region's countries were emerging from years of brutal and repressive military dictatorship, many of them backed by the United States. The new electoral systems were often rigid, exclusive and corrupt. However, rather than bringing about necessary reforms, Chavez created a system that has completely corrupted the electoral system, institutionalized massive corruption, criminalized nonviolent dissent, and made common cause with transnational terrorist and drug trafficking organizations. Beginning with the Chavez government and continuing into the Maduro administration Venezuela has actively pursued an official military doctrine that embraces the use of weapons of mass destruction against the United States.[3]

The stakes in the unfolding crisis in Venezuela for U.S. interests and the survival of democracy in Latin America are high. The consequences of the growth of the poisonous Bolivarian criminal enterprise are lethal.

Few understood this better than Alberto Nisman, the courageous Argentine prosecutor who was investigating the 1994 Iran-backed bombing of the AMIA Jewish center in Buenos Aires. Before being murdered on January 18 Nisman had documented the Bolivarian-Iran actions across the Western Hemisphere, including two attempted attacks backed by Iran in the United States. The week before his death, Nisman had formally accused Argentine President Cristina Fernandez de Kirchner and senior members of her inner circle of illegally seeking to cut to hide Iran's role in the AMIA case in exchange for oil to relieve Argentina's chronic fuel shortages. The warming relationship between Iran and Argentina was directly brokered by Venezuelan leaders. Whether or not the Argentine or Iranian government had direct roles in the unsolved murder of Nisman, the three nations together clearly created a climate in which he could be killed with impunity.[4]

As the Veja investigation shows, Venezuela was a key player in the efforts of Iran to reestablish nuclear ties to Argentina, and that such a relationship was of primary interest to the Iranians.[5] Because of the high value Iran placed on the acquisition of nuclear technology, Chavez promised to personally request Argentina's help, and to do so immediately.[6]

In addition nuclear overtures, Venezuela and Argentina have developed an elaborate and opaque mechanism for transferring millions of dollars in funds between the two nations with no oversight or accountability. One of the primary mechanisms was a program called "200 Socialist Factories," (200 Fabricas Socialistas). Venezuelan Government documents show that this program, although producing few functioning factories and even fewer economic benefits, allowed for direct Iranian participation in the ventures, most likely as a way of moving money that otherwise would be frozen under international financial sanctions.[7]

Of concern to the United States should be the stated policy of the Bolivarian bloc of nations to break the traditional ties of the region to the United States. To this end, the Bolivarian alliance has formed numerous organizations and military alliances—including a military academy in Bolivia to erase the vestiges of U.S. military training—which explicitly exclude the United States.[8]

U.S. influence is being replaced by a lethal doctrine of asymmetrical warfare, inspired by authoritarian governments seeking perpetual power and nurtured by Iran. Through an interlocking and rapidly expanding network of official Web sites, publishing houses, think tanks and military academies, the governments of Venezuela, Argentina, and Cuba have created a dominant narrative that identifies the United States as the primary threat to Latin America.

A constant in the narrative, and a particular favorite of the late Chavez, is that a U.S. invasion is imminent and unavoidable. This is because the alleged United States policy is based on pillaging the region's natural resources, toppling the revolutionary regimes leading the march to Latin American independence, and subjugating its citizens. This preposterous narrative is often used by Maduro to justify the repressive and illegal arrest of opposition leaders who are held for months and years without trial or charges, as alleged accomplices in the fabricated crimes.

This narrative has long been a part of the Latin American landscape, shaped by mass movements, armed insurgencies and Marxist ideologies, and based on the turbulent history of relations between the United States and the region. What is different now is the overt multigovernment sponsorship of the effort and the official adoption of these positions as policy and doctrine. This gives the current campaign deeper roots and access to levers of state power.

As discussed at length below, Iran, identified by successive U.S. administrations as a state sponsor of terrorism, has expanded its political alliances, diplomatic presence, trade initiatives, and military and intelligence programs in the Bolivarian axis, primarily through the deep ties with Venezuela.

In 2012 the United States intelligence community assessed that Iranian leadership was more willing to launch a terrorist attack inside the Homeland in response to perceived threats from the United States.[9]

In 2013 the Argentine prosecutor Nisman released a report documenting through little-studied reports, informants, and the Iranian media, how official Iran state policy embraced assassination and terror, something which it never tried to hide and has never recanted, and the role of Venezuela in Iran's strategy.

Many of the assumptions undergirding Prosecutor Nisman's work were drawn directly from the Iranian Constitution, an extraordinary document in which Iran stakes its claim to world domination in the name of Allah. It is worth a somewhat extended review here, given the repeated statements of solidary with Iran and its revolution by Venezuelan leaders. The preamble to the Iranian Constitution states:

> With due consideration for the Islamic Element of the Iranian Revolution, which has been a movement for the victory of all oppressed peoples who are confronted with aggressors, the constitution shall pave the way for perpetuation of this revolution within and outside the country, particularly in terms of the expansion of international relationships with other Islamic and popular movements. The Constitution seeks to lay the groundwork for the creation of a single world nation . . . and perpetuate the struggle to make this nation a reality for all the world's needy and oppressed nations.

It goes on to say that:

> In establishing and equipping the country's defense forces, we will allow for the fact that faith and ideology constitute the foundation and the criterion we must adhere to. Therefore, the army of the Islamic Republic of Iran and troops of the Revolutionary Guard will be created in accordance with the objective mentioned above, and will be entrusted with the task not only of protecting and preserving our borders, but also an ideological mission, that is to say, Jihad in the name of Allah and the world.[10]

Shortly after Nisman's 2013 report the U.S. Department of State issued a congressionally mandated report on Iran's activities in Latin America which completely ignored Nisman's fieldwork, as well as dissenting views within the U.S. government—most notably U.S. Southern Command, which has military responsibility for the region. Instead the State Department concluded that, while Iran's interest in Latin America "is of concern," Iranian "influence in Latin America and the Caribbean is waning."[11] In September 2014 the Government Accountability Office (GAO) issued a sharp critique of the State Department effort, noting the report only fully addressed 2 of the 12 issues raised, while partially addressing 6 issues, and leaving 4 completely unaddressed.[12]

In addition to serving as a gateway for Iran's presence in the region, Venezuela has also been the primary conduit for Russia's growing presence in the region, something of growing concern.

Riding on the wave of radical anti-U.S. populism sponsored by Venezuela, Russia is now firmly allied with the ranks of Latin America's populist, authoritarian and virulently anti-American leaders of the Bolivarian Alliance for the Peoples of Our America—(Alianza Bolivariana para los Pueblos de Nuestra América—ALBA). The Putin government is providing ALBA nations with weapons, police and military training and equipment, nuclear technology, oil exploration equipment, financial assistance, and an influential friend on the United Nations Security Council and other international forums.

In return, these allies are shielding Russia from international isolation, providing political and diplomatic support, and an important regional media network—both traditional and social—that offers unstinting support for Putin while casting the United States as the global aggressor. At the same time, ALBA countries are increasing Russia's access to the hemisphere's ports and airspace, and ultimately, increasing Russia's sphere of influence in a region where the United States has seldom been so challenged.[13]

Gen. John Kelly, the commander of the U.S. Southern Command, in his 2015 testimony before Congress, noted Russia's growing activities in Latin America were part of a global strategy of using "power projection in an attempt to erode U.S. leadership and challenge U.S. influence in the Western Hemisphere . . . Russia has courted Cuba, Venezuela and Nicaragua to gain access to air bases and ports of supply for Russian naval assets and strategic bombers operating in the Western Hemisphere."[14]

Where the Russian state establishes a presence, Russian organized crime invariably follows. The immediate consequence is the rapid increase in cocaine flows from Latin America to Russia, and the former Soviet Union, with almost all of the cocaine originating from countries that Russia vehemently supports—Venezuela, Nicaragua, Ecuador, and Bolivia.[15]

The FARC,[16] the hemisphere's oldest and largest insurgency and designated drug trafficking and terrorist organization by both the United States and European Union[17], remains at the center of a multitude of criminal enterprises and terrorist activities that stretch from Colombia south to Argentina, and northward to Central America and into direct ties to the Mexican drug cartels, primarily the Sinaloa organization. Despite ongoing peace talks with the government over the past 2 years, the insurgency remains involved in the massive laundering of drug money, and recent cases by the Drug Enforcement Administration (DEA) have shown the direct and growing criminal drug ties of the FARC and Hezbollah.

Following the model pioneered by Iran and Hezbollah, senior Venezuelan military and political leaders have allowed the FARC to traffic cocaine through Venezuela to West Africa, sharing in the profits. Almost every major shipment of cocaine to West Africa that U.S. law enforcement officials have been able to trace back have originated from or passed through Venezuelan territory.[18]

Under the protection of the Governments of Venezuela, Ecuador, Nicaragua and Bolivia—as well as powerful friends in El Salvador and Panama—the FARC maintains a robust international infrastructure that is producing and moving thousands of kilos of cocaine and laundering hundreds of millions of dollars. It has emerged as a pioneer hybrid criminal-terrorist insurgency, using drug money to sustain an ideological movement. Over time the ideology has faded and the FARC has become much more of a business enterprise, helping to enrich its leadership and the leadership of the regional governments it supports.

As one study of internal FARC documents, noted: "When Chavez became President of Venezuela in February 1999, FARC had not only enjoyed a relationship with him for at least some of the previous seven years but had also penetrated and learned how to best use Venezuelan territory and politics, manipulating and building alliances with new and traditional Venezuelan political sectors, traversing the Colombia-Venezuela border in areas ranging from coastal desert to Amazonian jungle and building cooperative relationships with the Venezuelan armed forces. Once Chavez was inaugurated, Venezuelan border security and foreign policies shifted in the FARC's favor."[19]

In this context there is also growing evidence that the Venezuela Government under Chavez and Maduro is actively promoting drug trafficking and TOC/terrorist groups, particularly the FARC and Hezbollah.[20] Perhaps the strongest public evidence of the importance of Venezuela to the FARC is the public designation of three of senior government officials by the U.S Treasury Department's Office of Foreign Assets Control (OFAC).

OFAC said the three—Hugo Armando Carvajal, director of Venezuelan Military Intelligence; Henry de Jesus Rangel, director of the Venezuelan Directorate of Intelligence and Prevention Services; and Ramon Emilio Rodriguez Chacin, former Minister of Justice and former Minister of Interior—were responsible for "materially supporting the FARC, a narcoterrorist organization." It specifically accused Carvajal and Rangel of protecting FARC cocaine shipments moving through Venezuela, and said Rodriguez Chacin, who resigned his government position just a few days before the designations, was the "Venezuelan Government's main weapons contact for the FARC."[21]

In November 2010, Rangel was promoted to the overall commander of the Venezuelan Armed Forces [22] and in January 2012 was named Defense Minister as part of Chavez's promotion of close associates tied to drug trafficking and the FARC.[23] In July 2014 Carvajal was detained in Aruba because of a U.S. indictment against him for drug trafficking in support of the FARC. Aruban authorities released him before he could be extradited. He received as a conquering hero when he returned to Venezuela.[24]

As legendary Manhattan district attorney Robert M. Morgenthau warned as he left public service in 2009 after decades of public service, including pursuit of numerous (and ongoing) criminal investigations into the Chavez government's role in TOC: ". . . [L]et there be no doubt that Hugo Chavez leads not only a corrupt government but one staffed by terrorist sympathizers. The government has strong ties to narcotrafficking and money laundering, and reportedly plays an active role in the transshipment of narcotics and the laundering of narcotics proceeds in exchange for payments to corrupt government officials."[25]

OFAC charges were buttressed by three other developments: A public presentation of Colombian intelligence on FARC camps in Venezuela and the meeting of high-level FARC commanders with senior Venezuelan officials, delivered at a session of the Organization of American States in July 2010; [26] the public release of an analysis of all the FARC documents—captured by the Colombian military from the March 1, 2008, killing of senior FARC commander Raul Reyes—by a respected British security think that outlined some of the same ties; [27] and the public statements of Walid Makled, a Venezuelan who was formally designated a drug kingpin by the U.S. Government.

Arrested by Colombian police after he fled Venezuela, Makled was eventually extradited back to Venezuela. Preet Bharara, U.S. Attorney for the Southern District of New York, dubbed Makeld, also known as ''The Turk,'' a ''king among kingpins.'' While in Colombian custody Makled gave multiple interviews and showed documents that he claimed showed he acquired control of one of Venezuela's main ports, as well as an airline used for cocaine trafficking, but paying millions of dollars in bribes to senior Venezuelan official.

According the U.S. indictment against him, Makled exported at least 10 tons of cocaine a month to the United States by keeping more than 40 Venezuelan generals and senior government officials on his payroll. ''All my business associates are generals. The highest,'' Makled said. ''I am telling you, we dispatched 300,000 kilos of coke. I couldn't have done it without the top of the government.'' [28] What added credibility to Makled's claims were the documents he presented showing what appear to be the signatures of several generals and senior Ministry of Interior officials accepting payment from Makled. ''I have enough evidence to justify the invasion of Venezuela'' as a criminal state, he said.[29]

There is growing evidence of the merging of the Bolivarian Revolution's criminal-terrorist pipeline activities and those of the criminal-terrorist pipeline of radical Islamist groups (Hezbollah in particular) supported by the Iranian regime. The possibility opens a series of new security challenges for the United States and its allies in Latin America.

Among the cases that provide evidence of these ties are:

- In 2008, OFAC designated senior Venezuelan diplomats for facilitating the funding of Hezbollah.

  One of those designated, Ghazi Nasr al Din, served as the charge d'affaires of the Venezuelan Embassy in Damascus, and then served in the Venezuelan Embassy in London. According to the OFAC statement in late January 2008, al Din facilitated the travel of two Hezbollah representatives of the Lebanese Parliament to solicit donations and announce the opening of a Hezbollah-sponsored community center and office in Venezuela. The second individual, Fawzi Kan'an, is described as a Venezuela-based Hezbollah supporter and a ''significant provider of financial support to Hezbollah.'' He met with senior Hezbollah officials in Lebanon to discuss operational issues, including possible kidnappings and terrorist attacks.[30]
- In April 2009, police in the island country of Curacao arrested 17 people for alleged involvement in cocaine trafficking with some of the proceeds being funneled through Middle Eastern banks to Hezbollah.[31]
- A July 6, 2009, indictment of Jamal Yousef in the U.S. Southern District of New York alleges that the defendant, a former Syrian military officer arrested in Honduras, sought to sell weapons to the FARC—weapons he claimed came from Hezbollah and were to be provided by a relative in Mexico.[32]

Such a relationship between nonstate and state actors provides numerous benefits to both. In Latin America, for example, the FARC gains access to Venezuelan territory without fear of reprisals; it gains access to Venezuelan identification documents; and, perhaps most importantly, access to routes for exporting cocaine to Europe and the United States—while using the same routes to import quantities of sophisticated weapons and communications equipment. In return, the Venezuelan Government offers state protection, and reaps rewards in the form of financial benefits for individuals as well as institutions, derived from the cocaine trade.

Iran, whose banks, including its central bank, are largely barred from the Western financial systems, benefits from access to the international financial market through Venezuelan, Ecuadoran, and Bolivian financial institutions, which act as proxies by moving Iranian money as if it originated in their own, unsanctioned financial systems.[33] Venezuela also agreed to provide Iran with 20,000 barrels of gasoline per day, leading to U.S. sanctions against the state petroleum company.[34]

There is now a significant body of evidence showing the FARC's operational alliance with Hezbollah and Hezbollah allies based in Venezuela under the protection of the Maduro government, to which relatively little attention has been paid.

A clear example of the breadth of the emerging alliances among criminal and terrorist groups was Operation Titan, executed by Colombian and U.S. officials beginning in 2008. Colombian and U.S. officials, after a 2-year investigation, dismantled a drug trafficking organization that stretched from Colombia to Panama, Mexico, West Africa, the United States, Europe and the Middle East. The operation then continued on for several more years as part of the *Lebanese-Canadian National Bank* case.

Colombian and U.S. officials say that one of the key money launderers in the structure, Chekry Harb, AKA ''Taliban'' acted as the central go-between among

Latin American drug trafficking organizations (DTOs) and Middle Eastern radical groups, primarily Hezbollah. Among the groups participating together in Harb's operation in Colombia were members of the Northern Valley Cartel, right-wing paramilitary groups and the FARC.

While there has been little public acknowledgement of the Hezbollah ties to Latin American transnational organized crime (TOC) groups, recent indictments based on DEA cases point to the growing overlap of the groups. In December 2011, U.S. officials charged Ayman Joumaa, an accused Lebanese drug kingpin and Hezbollah financier, of smuggling tons of U.S.-bound cocaine and laundering hundreds of millions of dollars with the Zetas cartel of Mexico, while operating in Panama, Colombia, the DRC and elsewhere.

"Ayman Joumaa is one of top guys in the world at what he does: international drug trafficking and money laundering," a U.S. antidrug official said. "He has interaction with Hezbollah. There's no indication that it's ideological. It's business." [35] Joumaa was tied to broader case of massive money laundering case that led to the collapse of the Lebanese Canadian Bank, one of the primary financial institutions used by Hezbollah to finance its worldwide activities.

Another little-studied aspect of Venezuela's vast financial network is the use of PDVSA, the state oil company, to move hundreds of millions of dollars, with no legal financial backing, through its friends and allies in the Petrocaribe association, which was established by Chavez as a way to provide subsidized oil to poorer countries in the region. Under the construct, the receiving country is supposed to pay for 50 percent of the oil deliveries at market prices on delivery and pay for the other 50 percent over a 22-year period at a 2-percent interest rate.

Yet the numbers don't add up in Central America's strongest Bolivarian members, Nicaragua and El Salvador. Hundreds of millions of dollars are received and spent with no auditing, no accountability and generally no trace.

The decision made by the leadership of the governing Sandinista party (FSLN)in Nicaragua and the governing Farabundo Marti (FMLN) in El Salvador, to work with the ALBA bloc of nations [36] and their nonstate allies such as the FARC in Colombia to move hundreds of millions of dollars in untraceable ways through interconnected state oil companies, sets them apart from other Central American nations. While Venezuela's oil exports plummet and the price of oil has collapsed, these two governments receive ever-larger amounts of cash that is untraceable.

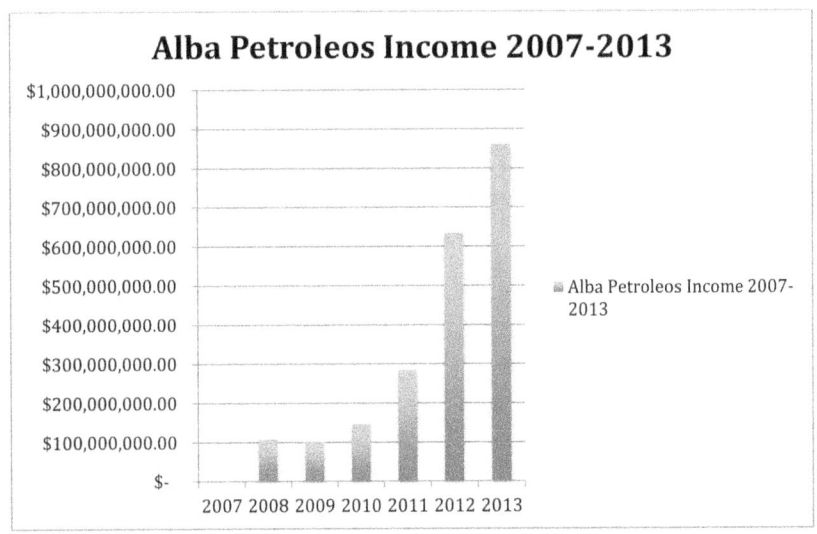

Figure 1: Earnings reported by ALBA Petróleos in El Salvador, which is 60 percent owned by Venezuela's PDVSA, showing an enormous and unjustified growth in income over seven years.

In El Salvador, the governing FMLN controls ALBA Petroleos, which is 60 percent owned by PDVSA. President Salvador Sanchez Ceren is a member of the ALBA leadership and former guerrilla commander with close ties to the FARC. According to public statements of FMLN leaders such as Jose Luis Merino, [37] ALBA Petroleos began with $1 million from PDVSA in 2007 and by the end 2013 had revenues of $862 million, with no explanation for the massive growth.[38] Merino, who is a senior ALBA Petroleos advisor, publicly stated that he knew that ''many people are nervous because ALBA Petroleos was born 6 or 7 years ago with $1 million and now has $400 million. Let me correct myself, $800 million, and we are trying to change the lives of Salvadorans.''[39]

Figure 2: Salvadoran President Salvador Sánchez Cerén (center) with FARC leader Manuel Marulanda (immediate left) and Raúl Reyes (immediate left, in camouflage) at a FARC camp in 2001.

One of the signature programs of ALBA in Nicaragua was to have been the construction of a large oil refinery. Named the ''Supreme Dream of Bolivar'' (Sueño Supremo de Bolívar), the refinery received $32 million in startup funding in 2008 and an additional $60 million over the following 3 years. In 2012 the program received an additional $141.2 million.

Yet all that is visible of the $237.2 million dollar investment is an empty field of compact earth with the flagstaffs bearing the flags of Nicaragua, Venezuela, Cuba, and ALBA. Construction machinery has remained idle at the site for 3 years.[40]

Figure 3: The empty field where $237.2 million have reportedly been spent over the past five years to build an as-yet invisible oil refinery. La Prensa (Nicaragua)

These last few cases, though far afield from Venezuela, constitute a key part of Venezuela's reach across the hemisphere and its ability to create corrupt structures, move well over $1 billion a year in unaccounted funds, and support criminal and terrorist organizations. These massive financial flows serve to corrupt the state, shield officials from accountability, create enormous "slush funds" for the governments to act without transparency, and are undermine the rule of law. They may also be of significant aid to drug trafficking and terrorist organizations.

As I noted earlier, Venezuela's ongoing state-sponsored criminal activities and ties to terrorist organizations are not confined to Venezuela. Rather, Venezuela has made itself the hub of a multinational criminal enterprise that has tentacles across the hemisphere, and that receives the active support of Iran, Russia and other nations that have a declared hostile intent toward the United States. This is the direct threat posed by Venezuela and its ongoing crisis.

End Notes

[1] Leonardo Courinho, "Chavistas confirmam conspiracao denuciada por Nisman," Veja, March 14, 2015.

[2] This definition is drawn from my study of transnational organized crime in Latin America. For a full discussion see: Douglas Farah, Transnational Organized Crime, Terrorism, and Criminalized States in Latin America: An Emerging Tier-One National Security Priority (Carlisle, PA: Strategic Studies Institute, U.S. Army War College, August 2012).

[3] The primary text outlining this philosophy, from which Chavez adopted his military doctrine is Peripheral Warfare and Revolutionary Islam: Origins, Rules and Ethics of Asymmetrical Warfare (Guerra Periférica y el Islam Revolucionario: Orígenes, Reglas y E tica de la Guerra Asimétrica) by the Spanish politician and ideologue Jorge Verstrynge. The tract is a continuation of and exploration of convicted terrorist Ilich Sanchez Ramirez's thoughts, incorporating an explicit endorsement of the use of weapons of mass destruction to destroy the United States. Verstrynge argues for the destruction of United States through series of asymmetrical attacks like those of 9/11, in the belief that the United States will simply crumble when its vast military strength cannot be used to combat its enemies.

Although he is not a Muslim, and the book was not written directly in relation to the Venezuelan experience, Verstrynge moves beyond Sanchez Ramirez to embrace all strands of radical Islam for helping to expand the parameters of what irregular warfare should encompass, including the use of biological and nuclear weapons, along with the correlated civilian casualties among the enemy.

[4] For a fuller discussion of the Nisman murder see: Douglas Farah, "The Murder of Alberto Nisman: How the Government of Cristina Fernandez de Kirchner created the environment for a perfect crime," International Assessment and Strategy Center, March 2015. For a fuller discussion of the triangulation efforts of Iran, Venezuela and Argentina in the nuclear program, see: Courihno, op cit.; Douglas Farah, "Back to the Future: Argentina Unravels," International Assessment and Strategy Center, February 2013.

[5] It is important to remember that throughout the 1970s until 1993 Argentina had a robust nuclear relationship with Iran, and the current Iranian reactors were retrofitted and upgraded with Argentine nuclear technology. Nisman, in his indictment of Iranian leaders for planning the AMIA bombing, stated that a major trigger for Iran's decision to blow up the AMIA building was the decision by Argentina, under pressure from the U.S. and Europe, to pause its nuclear

cooperation with Iran. In addition to the Veja article, see: Kaveh L. Afrasiabi, "Iran Looks to Argentina for nuclear fuel," Asia Times, November 6, 2009.

[6]Courinho, op. cit.

[7]Documents in possession of the author.

[8]These include recently founded Community of Latin American and Caribbean States (Comunidad de Estados Latinoamericanos y Caribeños-CELAC), and the Bolivarian Alliance for the Peoples of Our America (Alianza Bolivariana para los Pueblos de Nuestra América-ALBA).

[9]James R. Clapper, Director of National Intelligence, "Unclassified Statement for the Record: Worldwide Threat Assessment of the U.S. Intelligence Community for the Senate Select Committee on Intelligence, January 31, 2012, p. 6.

[10]Translation of the Iranian Constitution of 1979 provided by the University of Nevada Las Vegas.

[11]U.S. Department of State, "Annex A: Unclassified Summary of Policy Recommendations," June 2013. Most of the seven-page report was classified.

[12] United States Government Accountability Office, "Combatting Terrorism: Strategy to Counter Iran in the Western Hemisphere Has Gaps that State Department Should Address," September 2014, p. 8.

[13]Douglas Farah and Liana Eustacia Reyes, "Russia in Latin America: A Strategic Challenge," University of Miami, Center for Hemispheric Policy, January 15, 2015.

[14]"Posture Statement of General John F. Kelly, United States Marine Corps, Commander United States Southern Command Before the 114th Congress Senate Armed Services Committee," March 12, 2015.

[15]For the most comprehensive look at Russian Organized Crime in Latin America, see: Bruce Bagley, "Globalization, Ungoverned Spaces and Transnational Organized Crime in the Western Hemisphere: The Russian Mafia," paper prepared for International Studies Association, Honolulu, Hawaii, March 2, 2005.

[16]"Fuerzas Armadas Revolucionarias de Colombia" (Revolutionary Armed Forces of Colombia).

[17]"FARC Terrorist Indicted for 2003 Grenade Attack on Americans in Colombia," Department of Justice Press Release, September 7, 2004, and: Official Journal of the European Union, Council Decision of Dec. 21, 2005.

[18]Author interviews with Drug Enforcement Administration and National Security Council officials. For example two aircraft carrying more than 500 kilos of cocaine that were stopped in Guinea Bissau after arriving from Venezuela. See: "Bissau Police Seize Venezuelan cocaine smuggling planes," Agence France Presse, July 19, 2008.

[19]"The FARC Files: Venezuela, Ecuador and the Secret Archives of 'Raul Reyes,' " International Institute for Strategic Studies," May 2011.

[20]The strongest documentary evidence of Chavez's support for the FARC comes from the Reyes documents, which contained the internal communications of senior FARC commanders with senior Venezuelan officials, discussing everything from security arrangements in hostage exchanges to the possibility of joint training exercises and the purchasing of weapons. For full details of these documents and their interpretation, see: "The FARC Files: Venezuela, Ecuador and the Secret Archives of 'Raul Reyes,' " op cit.

[21]"Treasury Targets Venezuelan Government Officials Support of the FARC," U.S. Treasury Department Office of Public Affairs, Sept. 12, 2008. The designations came on the heels of the decision of the Bolivian Government of Evo Morales to expel the U.S. Ambassador, allegedly for supporting armed movements against the Morales government. In solidarity, Chavez then expelled the U.S. Ambassador to Venezuela. In addition to the designations of the Venezuelan officials, the United States also expelled the Venezuelan and Bolivian Ambassadors to Washington.

[22]"Chavez Shores up Military Support," Stratfor, November 12, 2010.

[23] "Venezuela: Asume Nuevo Ministro De Defensa Acusado de Narco por EEUU," Agence France Presse, January 17, 2012.

[24]"Venezuela gives 'hero's welcome' to freed Carvajal," BBC News, July 28, 2014.

[25]Robert M. Morgenthau, "The Link Between Iran and Venezuela: A Crisis in the Making," speech at the Brookings Institution, September 8, 2009.

[26]"Colombia, Venezuela: Another Round of Diplomatic Furor," Strafor, July 29, 2010.

[27]The FARC Files: "Venezuela, Ecuador and the Secret Archives of 'Raul Reyes,' " An IISS Strategic Dossier, International Institute for Strategic Studies, May 2011.

[28]The Colombian decision to extradite Makled to Venezuela rather than the United States caused significant tension between the two countries and probably means that the bulk of the evidence he claims to possess will never see the light of day. Among the documents he presented in prison were checks of his cashed by senior generals and government officials and videos of what appear to be senior government officials in his home discussing cash transactions. For details of the case see: Jose de Cordoba and Darcy Crowe, "U.S. Losing Big Drug Catch," The Wall Street Journal, April 1, 2011; "Manhattan U.S. Attorney Announces Indictment of one of World's Most Significant Narcotics Kingpins," United States Attorney, Southern District of New York, November 4, 2010.

[29]"Makled: Tengo suficientes pruebas sobre corrupción y narcotráfico para que intervengan a Venezuela," NTN24 TV (Colombia), April 11, 2011.

[30]"Treasury Targets Hizbullah in Venezuela," United States Department of Treasury Press Center, June 18, 2008.

[31] Orlando Cuales, "17 arrested in Curacao on suspicion of drug trafficking links with Hezbollah," Associated Press, April 29, 2009

[32]United States District Court, Southern District of New York, The United States of America v Jamal Yousef, Indictment, July 6, 2009.

[33]For a look at how the Ecuadoran and Venezuelan banks function as proxies for Iran, particularly the Economic Development Bank of Iran, sanctioned for its illegal support of Iran's nuclear program, and the Banco Internacional de Desarrollo, see: Farah and Simpson, op cit.

[34] Office of the Spokesman, ''Seven Companies Sanctioned Under Amended Iran Sanctions Act,'' U.S. Department of State, May 24, 2011.

[35] Sebastian Rotella, ''Government says Hezbollah Profits From U.S. Cocaine Market via Link to Mexican Cartel,'' ProPublica, December 11, 2011.

[36] The name is derived from former Venezuelan President Hugo Chavez's desire to recreate the original country created by South American liberator Simon Bolivar, which included Venezuela, Colombia, Panama, Bolivia and Ecuador. Chavez dubbed his movement, which has relied heavily on the FARC both for financing and as a nonstate armed actor, the Bolivarian Revolution. The radical populist bloc is formally known as ALBA, the Bolivarian Alliance for the Peoples of Our America or Alianza Bolivariana Para los Pueblos de Nuestro America. It members include Venezuela, Ecuador, Bolivia, Nicaragua, Jamaica, the Dominican Republic and El Salvador.

[37] Merino, better known by his nom de guerre Ramiro Vasquez, was a Communist Party urban commando during El Salvador's civil war and carried out a number of high profile kidnappings both during and after the war. He was a well-known weapons provider to the FARC. His relationship with the FARC leadership, as well as the Chavez government, were well documented in captured FARC documents, where he is identified as ''Ramiro the Salvadoran.''

[38] These figures are taken from ALBA Petroleos official financial filings.

[39] ''José Luis Merino defiende a Alba Petróleos por ataques de ANEP,'' Verdad Digital, October 31, 2013.

[40] For an more comprehensive look at the refinery project and interesting graphics see: Jose Denis Curz, ''El Supremo Sueño de Bolívar no avanza,'' La Prensa (Nicaragua), March 25, 2013.

Senator RUBIO. Thank you, all three, for being here.

Let me start with you, Dr. Sabatini. I wanted to ask you why—you have shared in your testimony something that Senator Boxer brought up earlier, and that is the silence of communities in Latin America and in the Western Hemisphere to what is happening in Venezuela. You compared it to the Honduran case that occurred back in 2009, if I am correct, and how that was met. Why, in your mind, is—why the silence from virtually everyone in the hemisphere with the exception of President Santos who condemned a specific arrest. But why the silence?

Dr. SABATINI. It is a good question, Senator. I have several theories.

I think first there has occurred in the last 10 years a proliferation of new regional organizations, led primarily by Brazil. There is a South American union, UNASUR. Then there is the Latin American-Caribbean union, CELAC. Both of those are intended to sort of marginalize the United States from those discussions. And not to wax too academic here, but those institutions actually lack a fundamental element of a multilateral institution. They do not ask their member countries to surrender any part of their sovereignty for a larger collective good. If you look at their founding documents, if you look at their statements, they always talk about how national sovereignty is supreme.

So I actually think that we have gone backward in the region. We talk about popular sovereignty. We are back to the point when Latin American countries assert this principle of nonintervention, which can have very dangerous consequences because that principle of popular sovereignty evolved after World War II to protect the horrendous things that happened in Nazi Germany. So I think, first of all, there has been actually a philosophical institutional shift within the region.

Second, I think that the region simply does not want to have the United States involved, and it is actively seeking to marginalize to do that. To give an example and to refer to what was said earlier about the need for election observation, be very careful. UNASUR's election observation program explicitly says that they are there to accompany—to accompany—the electoral commission which, if your electoral commission is vitiated or politicized, means you are just going there as a rubber stamp. So it is very important who monitors those elections.

And on the last point, there is certainly a level of ideological sympathy and affinity with a number of these governments which is a shame because while I believe Dilma Rousseff and the PT may be genuinely leftist, even a social democratic government, basically Venezuela is a military government led by a group of thugs. But unfortunately, they cannot make that distinction.

And last point, there are also very tight economic relations between—Brazil benefits deeply from agricultural exports, investment in infrastructure, and other things that sort of have made it very, very difficult to break its ties with Venezuela.

Senator RUBIO. Dr. Sabatini, you also talked and touched upon the drug trade. And as we know, if you watch the flights that come out of Colombia and South America and inner Central America and ultimately are transited into the United States, many of them over-fly Venezuela. It is hard to believe that those flights are occurring without the knowledge of someone in Venezuela. In fact, the allegations and some of the proof is very clear that the Venezuelan Government actually allows these flights to pay for protection money in exchange for being able to use airspace in Venezuela. If you do not pay the protection money, you may be shot down. If you pay the protection money to either a corrupt individual or to the Maduro government, you can over-fly that airspace. Is that an accurate assessment of the role Venezuela is playing in the drug trade?

Dr. SABATINI. That is a very accurate assessment. If you look at a map, basically Venezuela is crosshatched by flights that are coming from Colombia or leaving from Venezuela mostly to go to West Africa but now increasingly going to the Caribbean, again raising two points. One is why Venezuela is—as you say, since it is so closely tied to the drug trade at a state level and particularly at a military level, why this is a security risk to the region. And so Brazil and other countries ignore what is going on at their own peril. They will be most affected. And not coincidentally, one of the highest per capita consumers of cocaine today is Brazil.

Senator RUBIO. Mr. Canton, you described a Venezuela where there is no freedom of expression, where there is no freedom of assembly and association, where there is a lack of any sort of judicial independence, where there are arrests and detentions of opponents of the government, where there is degrading and cruel treatment of those opponents when imprisoned. Going deeper than that, we know that if you are a member of the opposition, you have virtually no access to the airwaves, no independent press. They are denied things like bulk paper imports. So they cannot even print. You are forced to sell to owners that are friendly to the regime.

Just a moment ago, I struggled to get the Department of State of the United States to acknowledge that Venezuela was no longer a democracy. In essence, democracy is more than just elections. Why should I continue to consider what they have in Venezuela today as a democracy given the fact that beyond having an election, which may or may not be even valid in some cases because of manipulation of the ballot, all the other underlying conditions of a democracy are not present? In essence, there cannot be a democracy unless both sides have free and fair access to the people who vote. Is Venezuela still a democracy?

Mr. CANTON. That is an excellent question. It is more academic than practical to some extent.

Maduro is the President elected by the popular vote, and nobody can argue against that. Maybe someone can argue that the elections were not free and fair. That is a possibility because he won only for 1.5. But he was elected by the popular vote.

All the other conditions of democracy are not there. I completely agree with you on that aspect. There is no independence of the judiciary. Legislation is just a rubber stamp institution. And there is constantly violations of human rights in the country.

Senator RUBIO. I am sorry. Let me rephrase my question this way. And I get your point.

Let us assume—and I do not. I do not accept this, but let us assume that the election was free and fair. Is Nicolas Maduro today governing Venezuela as a democrat?

Mr. CANTON. No, absolutely not. And rather than using the word "democracy" that can give space for ambiguity, I would say there is absolutely no rule of law in Venezuela.

Senator RUBIO. So formally on paper and institutionally, Venezuela has a democratic form of government. In how it is being governed today, it is no longer being governed as a democracy.

Mr. CANTON. Correct.

Senator RUBIO. And then, Mr. Farah, I wanted to talk to you about the national security aspects of this. Actually before I go to you, let me just finish this with Mr. Canton.

I know you did not get to it or could not get to it in your written statement because of the limited amount of time. Can you briefly describe, as you wrote in your testimony, the conditions that Leopoldo Lopez now faces in captivity?

Mr. CANTON. Everybody in jail in Venezuela is in a very serious situation and very grave situation on personal integrity and right to life.

Senator RUBIO. Is he in solitary confinement?

Mr. CANTON. He is in solitary confinement. And only a few weeks ago, there was an attempt to get into his cell by a gang of thugs in the prison. Nothing, fortunately, happened. I spoke with Leopoldo's mother only a week ago. He is in okay condition, but being in a jail in Venezuela, everybody, and particularly Leopoldo Lopez, your life is at risk.

Senator RUBIO. Is he allowed visits from his family on a regular basis?

Mr. CANTON. Not on a very regular basis. His mother can visit him once in a while, as well as his wife, but it is not very regular.

Senator RUBIO. Mr. Farah, I wanted to talk about the national security components. First of all, I think it is important at the outset to point to something that you did, and that is that throughout the 1970s until 1993, Argentina had a robust nuclear relationship with Iran and the current Iranian reactors were retrofitted and upgraded with Argentine nuclear technology. That is accurate.

Mr. FARAH. Yes, sir.

Senator RUBIO. Can you describe the nexus that exists today in your mind between Argentina, Iran, and Venezuela?

Mr. FARAH. Well, I think that Iran desperately wants to get its nuclear program up and running, and until the 1994 AMIA bombing, there was a very close exchange program between Iranian scientists and Argentinean scientists, et cetera. Prosecutor Nisman identified the cutting off of that relationship under U.S. and European pressure in 1993 as the trigger factor that set off the AMIA bombing in Buenos Aires in 1994.

So when Iran needed to get back in the game or wanted desperately to get back in the game, they approached Venezuela, Hugo Chavez specifically, with Nestor Kirchner, Cristina's husband and predecessor, to begin opening the dialogue. As the recent Veja investigation shows, President Chavez said immediately, yes, let me do this, get on it.

Nestor Kirchner was not particularly interested. In 2009, with Cristina they revisited it, and there was a steady flow or there has been a steady flow of Argentine scientists, nuclear folks, going to Venezuela. My understanding, from talking to people very familiar with Argentina's nuclear program, is that Iran has been interested in trying to recruit the entire team of scientists. They do not ones or twos. They want an entire team. And they are simply not willing to go. So that has not happened yet.

But I think Venezuela was the necessary bridge to bring the Kirchner government into contact with Iran, and then you had the whole ongoing scandal with the memorandum of understanding and other things that happened in Argentina as a result of that growing closeness. And ultimately you have Prosecutor Nisman's accusation that the President Kirchner and her Foreign Minister and others had illegally agreed with Iran to get the Interpol red notices dropped against senior Iranian officials in exchange for oil, et cetera. And you end up with Prosecutor Nisman dead.

But I think that in that entire process, the main interlocutor, the bridge between Iran and Argentina, has been and was very active was Venezuela, particularly President Chavez while he was alive, and ongoing with President Maduro.

Senator RUBIO. Okay. So we have established that there is a nexus there.

Let me ask you about this group called the FARC, which is largely operational within Colombia. This is a drug trafficking, narcoguerilla group currently engaged in peace negotiations with the Colombian Government. But they do things like extortion and kidnapping and bombings and so forth, in addition to their narcotrafficking activities. Correct?

Mr. FARAH. Yes, sir. They are one of three organizations that is both designated as a major drug trafficking organization and a terrorist organization by the U.S. Government.

Senator RUBIO. So the FARC is treated by the United States Government as both a terrorist organization and a narcotrafficking organization. Do they not have a presence in Venezuela today, and if so, what is the nature of it?

Mr. FARAH. They have a significant presence. I think captured FARC documents beginning in 2008 with the death of Raul Reyes, the FARC commander who was killed in Ecuador—we got about 600 gigabytes of data for the first time on the internal FARC communications. And what was shocking in that—I worked with both the Colombian Government and others on analyzing a chunk of those documents. And what was really eye-opening was the intense level of senior contact between the FARC Secretariat, the General Secretariat, and not only President Chavez directly but his entire Cabinet including Diosdado Cabello, Maduro, and all the others who are still there and the very intense relationship at the same level with the Ecuadorian Government of Rafael Correa. Those were the two sort of really significant findings.

But you see there the Venezuelan Government not only gave them shelter, it offered to set up joint businesses with them. It helped finance many of their activities. It carried their political water for them as far as trying to set up these different front groups. It hosted their main front group, which is the Bolivarian— the CCB, Coordinadora Continental Bolivariana. And the founding documents are in the FARC documents that were captured where the FARC complains that no one knows that this front group is a FARC group, but they describe how it was founded in the basement of the Presidential palace with President Chavez personally present.

So it is a very, very organic link that goes to the highest levels, and there is nothing nonstate about that relationship. The FARC is viewed much like Iran views Hezbollah, as a matter of state policy, as a nonstate actor that responds directly to them.

Senator RUBIO. What about the links between Venezuela and Hezbollah?

Mr. FARAH. I think that you have seen over time something that was initially largely dismissed, thanks to the Drug Enforcement Administration and the cases that have become public over the last few years. You see very, very tight links. You have Imad Muginyah and other very specific cases where the Hezbollah operatives were buying cocaine from the FARC, and much of that money is ending up back in places like the Lebanese Canadian Bank that have since been closed because that money was detected.

And it is often not as direct a link as people I discuss with in the policy world would like to see, but the money in my mind—they say, well, are they card-carrying Hezbollah people that are buying the cocaine? Who cares? The money ends up in Hezbollah in accounts back in Lebanon. Does it really matter whether the person who brokered that deal with the FARC has an ID card that says ''FARC'' or whether he is sympathetic enough to move that money back to Hezbollah? In my mind there is no distinction necessary there. But it becomes a very intense policy debate within this administration over what constitutes Hezbollah. My argument is that you simply need to look where the money ends up and who benefited from it, and it does not matter who the intermediaries were, identified specifically as that group.

Senator RUBIO. And my last question is about the state-owned company, PDVSA, Petroleos de Venezuela. How does the Venezuelan Government under the Maduro regime use PDVSA as the source of influence, activity, laundering, et cetera? How is that entity used both in the region and around the world?

Mr. FARAH. Well, I think the Bank of Andorra findings are extraordinarily important because I have been hearing for the last 3 or 4 years that Andorra was where PDVSA siphoned its money into. They have incredibly tough bank secrecy laws, and nothing had come out for a significant period of time.

I think that PDVSA has become sort of the piggybank that no longer has much cash in it. But what you see is an architecture created around the region, particularly with Maduro's allies in Nicaragua, Daniel Ortega, and Salvador Sanchez Ceren, and the remnants of the Communist Party in El Salvador, where you have architectures built up in which no oil is actually moved, but which they use to launder hundreds of millions of dollars a year. And simply looking at the financials of those companies, they are absurd. There are almost no legal imports coming in.

For example, ALBA Petroleos in El Salvador began with $1 million as this joint state enterprise with PDVSA owning 60 percent of the company and ALBA Petroleos owning 40. They had $1 million in 2007. Their earnings statement for 2013 was $863 million with no visible legitimate imports. That is a rather significant increase in your earnings. Daniel Ortega has said publicly that he gets $500 million a year from PDVSA essentially as a personal slush fund. And they set up with that an architecture which allows the FARC, the Sinaloa Cartel, Hezbollah, many other groups to launder money through the architecture that PDVSA has established.

Senator RUBIO. Let me just ask you one more, and I alluded to this earlier, a law enforcement report about the use of shipments from Venezuela to Syria to send bulk cash, both cash raised from the Arab expatriate community but also cash collected through trafficking of drugs and exacting bribes from drug traffickers and that money being sent to Assad. Are you aware of that report? Are you aware of those allegations? And if not, would that surprise you knowing the nature of the regime?

Mr. FARAH. I have heard the allegations. I have not seen documentation on it. I think that given the fact that when Chavez was most active in his direct engagement with Iran, the direct flight they set up went from Caracas to Damascus to Tehran back to Caracas, it is clear that there is a very strong link. If you look at the literature, Chavez had a very robust relationship with Assad. That has not changed. Maduro does not have the money, but clearly he is carrying on the same commitments that Chavez entered into. And I think that we have seen numerous cases of massive amounts of bulk cash being shipped back usually on Iranian ships which are untraceable once they get to Iran, and that some of that money would end up with Assad is not remotely——

Senator RUBIO. Is there still a direct flight between Caracas and Tehran?

Mr. FARAH. No, sir. That ended in 2011.

Senator RUBIO. So my last question—and I do not know who to direct this to, but any of you feel free to answer. I asked at the end of the last panel about Cuba's influence in Venezuela or its presence in Venezuela. And while I was able to get admission that there is an outsized influence, I could not get them to admit that the Cubans were actually involved in directing or helping the Venezuelan regime, the Maduro regime, oppress their own people.

So let me just ask all of you to comment on both the size, the scope of the Cuban presence in Venezuela. I hear from Venezuelans that are traveling back and others that it is an extraordinary presence, that you cannot miss it. And secondly, the nature of that to the extent you are able to comment. I guess, Dr. Sabatini, if you have anything to add to that.

Dr. SABATINI. I will start first. It is real. And I am going to tell perhaps an anecdote which illustrates it. I have a regular annual dinner with Cubans in the U.N. mission who, as we all know, are spies. And one time I was sort of chiding them a little bit, saying it must be difficult to be a client-state of Venezuela because they are so incompetent. They, of course, took umbrage at being called a "client-state," and they pushed back. And I said, but yes, they cannot manage it. You guys are real professionals. You are good spies. You do things very well. And there was a long pause, and finally literally they said, yes, but we are training them, which I think is precisely the point.

They are training. They are deeply embedded in the intelligence services. They are deeply embedded in the foreign ministry. I love that they often talk about they are sharing sports trainers. I do not know what sports trainers are, but clearly that is a euphemism for something else that is there.

Of course, they also have the medical doctors which, by the way, helps underwrite the Cuban pharmaceutical industry. When I was recently on a trip to Cuba, something I had never thought of, is the doctors that are being sent to Venezuela are writing prescriptions for Cuban drugs that are then shipped. So it sort of also benefits the pharmaceutical industry in Cuba.

It is real, and as I say, I have a firsthand account that they are there to train and they are there to advise.

Mr. CANTON. I agree it is real. In the particular case of the Inter-American System of Human Rights, the information I had when I was at the Inter-American Commission of Human rights was that all the movement of Venezuela to withdraw from the Inter-American System of Human Rights was orchestrated by Cuba. And over the last 2 years, as you know, Venezuela left the Inter-American System for the Protection of Human Rights, and that was because Cuba initiated all the process.

Mr. FARAH. I would just add one thing. I agree with both of my colleagues. One of the things that the Cubans were brought in to do—and you see it not only in Venezuela but certainly in Bolivia and Ecuador, perhaps more pronounced because they are smaller societies—is that in those countries—and I grew up in Bolivia—if you were someone of stature and you got arrested, you had a social network that would get you out of prison. I never worried during the military dictatorships in Bolivia. If I was picked up—I was going to school with the sons of colonels—there was a social network that would get those people out.

The Cubans were brought in to break that social network. They do not care who your uncle went to school with. They do not care who you went to class with. They do not care about any of that. And that has facilitated in all three of these countries the ability to throw people like Leopoldo Lopez in prison with no social network that can mobilize to get them out. The Cubans were brought in to essentially slice through those existing sort of safety net cords that had survived through the dictatorships and helped a lot of people get sanctuary because they are beholden to no one and they know it and they can just tell you to walk away and that is it. So it is a very important function they play besides, as was pointed out, being incredibly active at the very senior levels.

Senator RUBIO. Well, I guess I ask all these questions because while a lot of people were taken aback by the language of the President's announcement last week that Venezuela poses a national security threat, perhaps a better way to have phrased it— and I understand they are constrained by bureaucratic necessities, but—is not that Venezuela poses a threat per se. The people of Venezuela have no animosity toward the United States, at least the vast majority, the enormous and overwhelming majority, and certainly do not pose a threat to the country.

But the Maduro regime, as has been described here today, is an anti-American one, is a serial human rights violator, is one that governs undemocratically. It is one that is helping—has and may continue to be helping Iran try to evade international sanctions and advance its nuclear program. It is one that is involved aiding both a terrorist and narco group called the FARC by giving them safe haven and support within their own territory. It is one that is involved, by the way, in openly providing safe passage for drug traffickers for drugs that are ultimately destined for the United States. It is one that actively supports financially Hezbollah, and it is one that uses its state-owned enterprise to foment and support anti-American governments in the region. And last by not least, it is one that is completely infected by a foreign government that has flooded it with sports trainers or, as they are more accurately known, spies and agents of repression that allow it to crack down on its own people and also further the interests of that country over that of the people of Venezuela.

That sounds like the Maduro regime is not an insignificant threat to the national security of the United States when you view it in this context. This is not just a nation that is failing economically because of incompetent leaders, and it is certainly that. But it is also one in the grips of a regime that actively supports global terrorism, that actively supports one of the most dangerous developments of the last 20 years, which is Iran's nuclear ambition, that actively supports a group that is both a narcoterrorism group and also just a flat-out terrorist group. It is one that represses its own people brutally with the assistance of the Cuban Government.

This does not sound to me like something that should be taken lightly despite the fact that it does not receive the attention it deserves. It does sound like not Venezuela, but the Maduro regime poses a real national security risk not just to the United States but to the region.

Would anyone disagree with that assessment or elaborate on it?

Mr. CANTON. I agree. But the issue is how to address that problem. And I believe it is better if the United States acts together with the other countries of the region, with the OAS, with UNASUR, not being alone. I am in agreement—we were discussing with Chris this before. I am in agreement with the sanctions, but it is important for the United States to have very active diplomacy with the OAS and UNASUR.

Over the next few months, there are very important issues happening in the region. There is a new change of the Secretary General of the OAS. The last Secretary General, Jose Miguel Insulza, failed during 10 years, his tenure at the OAS, at the same time of the destruction of democracy in Venezuela. There is the Summit of the Americas in just a couple of weeks, and there is the election internally in Venezuela.

So I think it is important for the United States to work together with the other countries of the region. I know it is not easy. I know it is not the best timing, but it is the best way to approach the situation in Venezuela.

Senator RUBIO. And, Mr. Canton, I would not disagree. I would love nothing more than to see the nations of the region condemn what is happening in Venezuela. I would love to see nothing more than at least one country, at least one, come forward and say what is going on in Venezuela is outrageous and as a neighboring country, we are outraged by it. The problem is that we have not seen any of that occur, and in the interim U.S. national security is at stake.

In fact, as Senator Menendez pointed earlier, about a year ago, the administration did not want to do sanctions because they wanted to give time for his UNASUR process to work. And the problem with that process, of course, was that they went in and basically treated both sides as moral equals when they were not. One side was unarmed civilians protesting conditions in Venezuela, and the other side were armed with sticks and clubs and guns and were beating them. And they also happened to have the power of government on their side.

So while I agree with you and I share with you the hope that we would be joined by other nations, recent history does not hold much hope that that is going to happen. And I think it is to the great shame of the nations in this hemisphere who stand by silently and are watching this happen.

Anyone else care to elaborate on my statement?

Mr. FARAH. I would fully agree. I wrote a paper that the Army War College published in 2012 saying that the criminalized states of Latin America should be considered a Tier 1 national security threat. And I think that that has been—because not only, as I said in my testimony, is it Venezuela, it is a network of countries now acting in concert with extra-regional actors with the primary unifying factor in all of their ideologies is a hatred for the United States and a firm belief in their public doctrine that the use of WMD against the United States is acceptable military doctrine and necessary military doctrine. I think because we do not take people seriously when they tell us what they want to do, that that is a serious oversight on our part, and that as they move forward, that strategic goal on their end has not changed.

Dr. SABATINI. I will just add quickly I agree with you. And for so long, this administration, which I support, has first talked about the new era of partnership in the hemisphere. The truth is partners do not treat partners like Brazil and others are treating us. They do not denounce—perhaps inflammatory language but an action that, in fact, they embraced only a few years earlier when it came to Honduras. I think we need to find who our allies are in the region and work with them carefully to find a comfort zone where they can start to engage in this because, I agree with you, Venezuela is a national security threat probably more to the region than it is the United States, which makes it all the ironic that they are the ones who are criticizing us for saying it.

Senator RUBIO. Well, I appreciate your insights today. I think, if anything, this hearing I hope will remind my colleagues and the American people about what we are facing in our own hemisphere. Number one is just an astronomical level of human rights abuses and an erosion of democracy which, by the way, is not only contained to Venezuela. You find that erosion of democracy in Bolivia and in Ecuador and in Nicaragua and certainly the total absence of it in Cuba. It is one of those startling new developments we have seen after 20 years of democratic progress where people come to power through an election and then immediately undermine all of the institutions necessary for a vibrant democracy. It is one we have ignored for far too long.

The second point is I hope people realize that in our own hemisphere there is a regime that is actively supporting and profiting from the trafficking of drugs that ultimately wind up in our streets, that is actively supporting, openly supporting elements that are both narcoterrorists but also just flat-out terrorists who have killed and maimed not just people in this region but oftentimes Americans, that in this region, there is a regime that is an active supporter of Iran's nuclear ambitions, that in this region, there is a regime surrounded by a level of enablers and cronies who steal all this money from the Venezuelan people, who benefit from access to power in Venezuela, and then spend weekends and holidays parading up and down the streets of Miami enjoying their ill-found gains.

So that is why I am supportive of the bill we passed last year and supportive of the President's decisions. And I hope people realize that all the problems of the world are not in the Middle East. All problems of the world are not only in Asia or in Europe. There are real and significant problems in our own hemisphere that impact life in America.

And the last point I hope people will take away from today is that we believe that the future of Venezuela belongs to the people of Venezuela. In a perfect and ideal world, the world that we are pushing toward, the Venezuelan people through the ballot box will replace these leaders with ones of their own choosing, which will help Venezuela fulfill its destiny as a prosperous, peaceful, and free country. That is not the direction it is headed in today.

And while we cannot mandate the conditions in Venezuela, nor should we try and that is not our intention to do so, we certainly should lift our voice anytime human rights are being violated, especially in such a grotesque manner, and we will certainly condemn those who are benefiting and profiting from these abuses and then coming to our own shores to enjoy those benefits from the money they have stolen from their own people.

And last but not least, we cannot ignore, despite the recent opening, the Cuban influence in Venezuela and the role that they are playing. Nicolas Maduro recently said that the United States was planning to invade Venezuela, which anyone familiar with United

States policy just knows how absurd it is and how ridiculous a statement that is. But I would say to you that there is an invasion going on in Venezuela and it is an invasion of Cubans—of Cuban agents and Cuban Government officials—that have infiltrated the highest levels of its government who provide personal protection to Nicolas Maduro and Chavez before him, who control the official documents of the government, who are training their sports department better known as their repressive regime. And these things are happening as well and it should give us insight into the true nature of the Cuban Government.

With that, again, I appreciate you being here today, your insights, the work that went into your statements.

The record is going to remain open until the close of business on Thursday, March 19, for any future submissions. You may receive questions from other members, and I would encourage you to answer those so we can get them officially in the record.

And with that, this hearing is adjourned.

[Whereupon, at 12:43 p.m., the hearing was adjourned.]

ADDITIONAL MATERIAL SUBMITTED FOR THE RECORD

WRITTEN STATEMENT OF MARIA EUGENIA TOVAR, A VENEZUELAN CITIZEN, SUBMITTED BY SENATOR MARCO RUBIO

Honorable Senators, my name is Maria Eugenia Tovar, Venezuelan citizen in the process of obtaining political asylum in this country because of the political persecution I suffered in Venezuela due to what happened to my daughter, Genesis Carmona Tovar, who was murdered in the city of Valencia, Carabobo State, Venezuela, by a gunshot to the head on February 18, 2014, while we were participating in a pacific protest. I would like to respectfully greet you, and to thank the United States Congress, for being able to pass the law, Venezuela Defense of Human Rights and Civil Society Act of 2014, sanctioning those who violated the human rights of the pacific demonstrators in Venezuela last February.

I respectfully ask the committee to process the inclusion of those who murdered Genesis Carmona Tovar, into the list of people sanctioned for ordering and doing these horrific crimes. This crime still goes unpunished.

On February 18 of 2014, I, Maria Eugenia Tovar, along with my children, Christian Carmona Tovar, who is 15 years old; Alejandra Carmona Tovar, 19 years old; and Genesis Carmona Tovar, 22 years old, were participating in the pacific demonstration in the Cedeno Avenue in the city of Valencia, Carabobo State, when we were caught by surprise by armed groups known as "Los Colectivos," who shot us, murdering my daughter, Genesis.

One of the people responsible of such a vile and despicable act is the governor of Carabobo State, Francisco Ameliach, who in his Twitter account, @ameliachpsuv, the day before Genesis was shot dead, wrote calling all members of the Unit of the Bolivar-Chavez Battle (UBCH) to prepare the "immediate counterattack" against the "fascists."

Besides Ameliach, members of the UBCH are also responsible. They are led by Samuel Martinez Garcia, bearer of the ID number 17,824,120, Coordinator of the "Juventud Partido Socialista Unido de Venezuela (Youth of the United Socialist Party of Venezuela), who lives in the 2nd Street, house number 2,neighborhood Guanabanillo, in the municipality of Juan Jose Mora, Carabobo State; and Juan Jose Maza Seijas, ID Number 19,425,960, leader of the oganization "Juventud del PSUV" (PSUV Youth) of Carabobo State, and a public official that works in the Ministry of Youth.

With an arrest warrant, only Juan Jose Maza Seijas appeared before a judge, once he got captured while he was staying in his residence. The district attorneys 44th and 146th of the Metropolitan Area of Caracas (AMC), Ruben Perez and Yackeline Mata, respectively, ratified the accusation against Maza Seijas due to his complicity in the felony of intentional homicide characterized with malice aforethought and ignoble motives, as well as his association to commit a crime.

The preliminary hearing was held in the Trial Court 36th of Control of the AMC, which admitted the introduction of the charges from the prosecutors, and ordered the trial of the Maza Seijas case, agreeing on an interim measure of a consistent presentation every 15 days before said judicial instance, requested by the above mentioned district attorneys and agreed on by the judge of the case.

However, the prosecutors, as well as the judge of this case acted by omission, leaving this case to go judicially unpunished. The duties of the prosecutors Perez and Mata were not held in accordance to their duty as guarantors of the due process; they did not continue with the judicial investigation to identify the hooded armed men that murdered Genesis Carmona; and considering the extent of such an aberrant crime, they should not have requested an interim measure to the judge. As prosecutors, they should have continued the process to make Samuel Martinez appear before the judge, but they did not do it. The judge, also, should have denied the interim measure, and do the necessary procedures, but he did not do it either.

Therefore, the prosecutors Ruben Perez and Yackeline Mata, as well as the judge of this case, should be held responsible for the impunity of the murder of Genesis Carmona, especially since Martinez and Maza still have their jobs at the Mayor's office, and they are enjoying full freedom.

In the following videos, it can be seen both men, who allowed themselves to be thoroughly identified in it, unhooded, and giving orders to hooded men to shoot and murder my daughter, Genesis Carmona Tovar:

www.youtube.com/watch?v=Humx3BvFQjo
www.youtube.com/watch?v=zX9Bx7iYzyU
www.youtube.com/watch?v=EOdDPTiriyM

Samuel Martinez Garcia, who appears in the video with long hair, and Jose Maza Seijas coordinate and manage the violent groups, the armed "Colectivos," whom have been dedicated to suppress the protests in Valencia.

Also, in the video the mayor, Maxum Caldera, and Guilmer Benitez were identified but never investigated. In that same event, 8 people were wounded.

I would like to mention Hector Breiia, Coordinator of Economic matters of the Governor's Office of the State of Carabobo and one of the most loyal for the dirty jobs of Governor Ameliach, who is another one of the leaders of the Collectives in Valencia and also he dedicates himself to persecute, threaten, track communications and order the monitoring of the opposition people he threatens with death. Mr. Breiia spent the December holidays of 2014 in the city of New York.

This case can be found, nowadays, in the Criminal Appellate Division of the Supreme Court of Justice (TSJ), where still nothing has happened.

Finding ourselves in the District of Senator Marco Rubio, and he being the person who represents us before the Senate, and knows this case thoroughly, we feel deeply grateful because he raised his voice before the corresponding bodies. We beg for you to follow up on this case, and help us bring it to justice, since in Venezuela this is not possible.

We are deeply grateful for having fulfilled the mission of passing the Venezuela Defense of Human Rights and Civil Society Act of 2014. Now, we are counting on your support so the Department of State can continue with the implementation and execution of this law, finding the culprits, and sanctioning them as violators of human rights.

We are absolutely certain that with the sanctions achieved by Congress all those guilty of the murder of Genesis Carmona will be sanctioned. And even though it does not fix the loss of her life, it would comfort us, the family members that hold the ideals of peace and justice.

————

RESPONSES OF ALEX LEE TO QUESTIONS SUBMITTED BY SENATOR MARCO RUBIO

Question. Mr. Lee, during this committee's last hearing on Venezuela in May 2014, Assistant Secretary Roberta Jacobson stated that "We do think that right now they (sanctions) would be counterproductive, that they would enable the Venezuelan Government to go back to that sort of victim mentality of using us. But there may well come a time at some point in the future when they would be useful if there has not been movement at the table."

- What has changed in Venezuela in the last 10 months that has made the administration feel now is the right time for targeted sanctions? Why did it take so long?
- What process did the administration use in picking who would be targeted for sanctions?

♦ Why are only seven names on the list?

♦ Are there additional members of the Venezuela Government who will be targeted in the future?

Answer. Over the course of the last year, we have taken several steps in response to human rights concerns in Venezuela. On July 30, 2014, and again on February 2, 2015, the Department imposed visa restrictions on certain Venezuelans believed to be responsible for, or complicit in, human rights abuses and undermining democratic governance. Certain family members of such individuals were also affected by these actions.

The Secretary of State took these steps pursuant to Section 212(a)(3)(C) of the Immigration and Nationality Act.

On March 9, 2015, the President issued an Executive order imposing sanctions on seven designated individuals and authorizing the Secretary of the Treasury to impose sanctions on additional individuals and entities, in part to implement the Venezuela Defense of Human Rights and Civil Society Act of 2014 (the ''Act''). The interagency culled through various public and nonpublic sources to identify candidates that meet the criteria provided for in the Executive order. These names were thoroughly vetted by the interagency.

When considering targeted measures, including visa restrictions or asset blocking, we routinely take into account a variety of factors including the particular facts of each case, the overall political context, law enforcement considerations, and consultations with our regional partners. We do not take such actions precipitously or without serious deliberation and they are always done consistent with relevant applicable laws or regulations.

We will continue our investigations pursuant to the authorities established by the Act and the President's Executive order and we stand prepared to take action against others, where appropriate, as we assess additional information.

Every situation is unique; our actions must be guided by the approach most likely to succeed in advancing respect for democracy and human rights for the benefit of the Venezuelan people.

Question. Recently, Venezuela has requested that the United States Embassy reduce its diplomatic staff to 17, to match their staff numbers in the Venezuelan Embassy in Washington.

♦ How many diplomatic personal does Venezuela have registered in the United States? (Consulate and Embassy)

♦ What is the latest development regarding Venezuela's request for the United States to develop a plan to downsize the U.S. Embassy to a staff of 17?

♦ What would be the impact of such a staff reduction on U.S. interests in Venezuela and services provided by the Embassy?

♦ What type of response is the State Department considering for Venezuela's diplomatic representation in the United States?

Answer. According to State Department records, Venezuela has 74 individuals accredited and/or registered with its Embassy and eight Consulates. On March 16, we sent a diplomatic note to the Venezuelan Government that extended an offer to send a team of technical experts to discuss the size of both our missions. We have not yet received a response. The size of the Venezuelan mission to the United States will be an important part of those discussions.

We have made clear to the Venezuelans that they need to comply with their international obligations to protect diplomats. Under the Vienna Convention on Diplomatic Relations, Venezuela committed to take steps to protect our diplomatic mission and our personnel at the mission, and the Department has made clear, and will continue to insist, that Venezuela provide such protection as the host government. A top priority for us remains the ability to ensure the welfare of American citizens in Venezuela. We will work to ensure the Embassy can continue to provide that assistance. Further, we have advised the Venezuelan Government that a reduction in our staff could negatively affect our ability to meet the demand for U.S. visas in Venezuela. It could also impact our public outreach efforts and the size and scope of cultural and educational exchanges.

Question. The ''Anti-Imperialist Enabling Law'' was passed by the Venezuelan Legislature on Sunday and gives President Nicolas Maduro the ability to enact laws without congressional authorization through the rest of this year.

♦ With the passage of the ''Anti-Imperialist Enabling Law,'' is President Nicolas Maduro now essentially Dictator Nicolas Maduro?

♦ Are there any checks on Maduro's power? Anything to prevent him from beginning mass arrest of opposition leaders?

◆Has there been any outcry from the international community about the gross injustice to the democratic process in that has just occurred?

◆Has any South American country called out for a return to democratic process?

Answer. We are concerned by the weakening of democratic institutions in Venezuela and have called for a clear separation of powers. Political interference in both the legislature and the judicial branch has undermined the ability of those institutions to provide a significant check on the Executive. There is a process in the Venezuelan Constitution for Venezuela's National Assembly to grant a Venezuelan President the power to rule by decree.

As underscored in the Inter-American Democratic Charter, which all democracies of the region have committed to uphold, the separation of powers and the independence of the branches of government are essential elements of representative democracy. An independent legislature has an essential role to play in the political system in order to meet the principles laid out in the Charter.

This year's National Assembly elections present an opportunity for Venezuelans to engage in legitimate, democratic discourse. Transparent election processes and credible election results could also reduce tensions in the country. We have urged regional partners to encourage Venezuela to accept a robust international electoral observation mission, using accepted international standards, for those elections. Now is the time for the region to cooperate and help Venezuela work toward a democratic and inclusive solution to the challenges it faces. We will also continue to work closely with others in the region to support greater political expression in Venezuela, and to encourage the Venezuelan Government to live up to its commitments to democracy and human rights, as articulated in the OAS Charter, the Inter American Democratic Charter, and other relevant instruments.

Foreign Ministers from the Union of South American Nations (UNASUR) released a March 14 statement announcing support for the upcoming parliamentary elections, the importance of the maintenance of the constitutional order, as well as democracy and the full expression of all human rights.

Question. To what extent is there genuine independence between the Venezuelan executive, legislative, and judiciary powers?

Answer. In Venezuela today, there is an increasingly authoritarian Executive exercising significant control over the legislative, judicial, and electoral branches of government as well as the human rights ombudsman.

As underscored in the Inter-American Democratic Charter, which all democracies of the region have committed to uphold, the separation of powers and the independence of the branches of government are essential elements of representative democracy. We will continue to work closely with others in the region to support greater political expression in Venezuela and to encourage the Venezuelan Government to live up to its required commitments to democracy and human rights, as articulated in the OAS Charter, the Inter American Democratic Charter, and other relevant instruments.

Question. Is Venezuela a democracy today?

Answer. Venezuela is formally a multiparty constitutional republic, but unfortunately, in recent years, political power has been concentrated in a single party with an increasingly authoritarian Executive exercising significant control over the legislative, judicial, and electoral branches of government as well as the human rights ombudsman. The government's actions have not met its required commitments to democracy and human rights, as articulated in the OAS Charter, the Inter American Democratic Charter, and other relevant instruments.

Question. Do you agree that financial and visa sanctions could be a strong deterrent against further brutality against demonstrators?

◆If so, why has the administration been so slow to deploy these tools as a deterrent?

Answer. Our efforts to sanction the individuals listed in the annex to the March 9 Executive order, and cut them off from the U.S. financial system, exposes their objectionable behavior. We hope this increased pressure will prompt authority figures to change their ways or face further isolation from the international community.

In addition, the United States is sending a clear message that it does not welcome money or travel of those who may be involved in human rights violations and abuses, undermining democratic governance, or engaging in public corruption.

The Department has stated in the past that a balanced approach toward targeted measures, including visa restrictions or asset blocking, must account for a variety of factors such as the overall political context, law enforcement considerations, and consultations with our regional partners. With that in mind, the Department first took steps to impose visa restrictions for certain Venezuelans believed to be responsible for, or complicit in, human rights abuses and undermining democratic governance, including public corruption on July 30, 2014, and again February 2, 2015. Certain family members of such individuals may also be affected by these actions.

Any sanctions efforts should be seen as a tool in the context of a broader diplomatic strategy that must include working with allies in the region, those defending democracy within countries, and partners outside the region as well as multilateral organizations.

Question. How many Active Duty military officers lead civilian agencies in the Government of Venezuela?

Answer. Currently, five out of Venezuela's 28 ministries are headed up by active military personnel, by our estimate. These military officers lead the ministries of the Presidency (Admiral Carmen Melendez Rivas); defense (General Vladimir Padrino Lopez); economy and finance (Brigadier General Rodolfo Clemente Marco Torres); interior, justice, and peace (Major General Gustavo Gonzalez Lopez); and aquatic and aerial transport (Mayor General Giuseppe Yoffreda). In his last Cabinet, President Hugo Chavez only had three active military officers, including the Defense Minister, although in some of his previous Cabinets, Chavez had as many as seven Active-Duty ministers.

President Nicolas Maduro has also appointed Active-Duty military officers to lead the National Police (General Manuel Eduardo Perez Urdaneta) and the state-run supermarket cooperatives, Mercal (Lieutenant Coronel Tito Gomez) and Abastos Bicentenarios (Major Anderson Medina). In addition to being Minister of Interior, Justice and Peace, Major General Gustavo Gonzalez Lopez also serves as the director general of the Bolivarian National Intelligence Service (SEBIN).

Question. How does that number [of Active-Duty military officers leading civilian agencies] compare to other countries in the Western Hemisphere?

Answer. Venezuela has one of the highest rates of Active-Duty military officers in civilian cabinet positions, according to our estimates. Most other countries in the region—with the exception of Cuba—have all civilian cabinets or only have military officers heading the Ministry of Defense or defense-related agencies.

Question. Does the Venezuelan military pose a threat to peace and the return of democracy in Venezuela?

Answer. Elected civilian authorities' decisions have led to the significant economic, social, and political challenges in Venezuela. We believe the long-term solution in Venezuela will require meaningful dialogue among Venezuelans that yields concrete results and this year's National Assembly elections are an important part of that process. In general, we believe civilian leadership should handle the civilian functions of a government along with overseeing a nation's military.

Question. Would you agree that, in Congress passing the "Venezuela Defense of Human Rights and Civil Society Act of 2014" (113–278) and in the President of the United States signing and implementing this law the United States acted entirely within its sovereign right to protect the integrity of its financial system and national security?

Answer. Yes, the United States, like all states, can decide who may use its financial system or enter its territory. Executive Order 13692 and the Venezuela Defense of Human Rights and Civil Society Act of 2014 embodied this decision by the United States in relation to individuals that meet the criteria for sanctions under those authorities. The visa restrictions and asset blocking against individuals who meet the criteria in the Executive order signaled that those Venezuelans who violate or abuse human rights or undermine democracy are not welcome in the United States, nor are they allowed to use our financial system. These actions made clear the U.S. Government's concerns about the erosion of human rights and democracy in Venezuela.

Question. Would you say that it is hypocritical for the United States to be criticized for acting within its sovereign rights while other countries hide behind this principle in order to avoid taking a stance regarding human rights in Venezuela?

Answer. We believe that all actors should focus their efforts on promoting democratic dialogue and free and fair elections in Venezuela. Other states and international organizations have highlighted the importance of democracy in the region and have called for Venezuela to respect democracy, human rights, and the rule of law.

The long list of international actors who have voiced concerns about the human rights situation in Venezuela over the past year includes the Governments of Colombia, Costa Rica, and Peru; the former Presidents of Brazil, Chile, Costa Rica, Mexico, Panama, Peru, and Uruguay; as well as respected international bodies such as the United Nations Committee against Torture, and the Secretary General of the Organization of American States.

Ultimately, Venezuela's political and economic problems will be solved by Venezuelans talking to one another in a climate of respect for human rights and democracy, and we should all encourage moves in that direction.

Question. Would you agree that the United States deserves the same respect for its sovereignty as other nations in the world, and specifically in the Western Hemisphere?

Answer. Yes.

Question. I find it hypocritical that the administration has supported sanctions in Venezuela but yet relaxed them in Cuba. We have seen the influx of Cuban military and state security in repressing activists in Venezuela. After Cuba's history of supporting violence in Latin America and Africa when it was heavily subsidized by the U.S.S.R.

♦ Does the administration want, by weakening sanctions against the Castro regime, to help that dictatorship spread its repression even more into Venezuela and beyond?

Answer. The United States imposes sanctions on both countries out of concern for human rights. But those sanctions are applied differently according to an evolving and unique set of challenges that each country presents.

We constantly reevaluate the implementation of these policies and whether we need to change our course. In the case of Venezuela, the new sanctions are aimed at persons involved in or responsible for the erosion of human rights guarantees, persecution of political opponents, curtailment of press freedoms, use of violence and human rights violations and abuses in response to antigovernment protests, and arbitrary arrest and detention of antigovernment protestors, as well as the significant public corruption by senior government officials in Venezuela. In the case of Cuba, the new measures allowing for greater travel and commerce are intended to support the ability of the Cuban people to gain greater control over their own lives and determine their country's future.

Question. According to high-level military defectors from Venezuela's Government, there are between 2,700 and 3,000 Cuban intelligence agents in the South American nation, embedded in sectors such as the military, agriculture, finance, and petroleum refining.

♦ Is this assessment correct?

♦ How many Cuban intelligence agents in Venezuela is the U.S. Government aware of?

Answer. Cuba and Venezuela have a long-standing and wide-ranging partnership. They cooperate in areas ranging from intelligence services to medical services. In light of the close ties between the two countries, it should come as no surprise that Cubans are involved in the military, agriculture, finance, and petroleum refining sectors. However, we are not able to comment in a public manner about the estimates of the number of Cuban intelligence agents in Venezuela that may be provided by Venezuelan defectors or other open sources.

Question. According to high-level military defectors from Venezuela's Government, the Cubans have modernized Venezuela's intelligence services, both the Sebin (Bolivarian National Intelligence Service) that reports directly to the President, and military intelligence. They also set up a special unit to protect Nicolas Maduro.

♦ Do you have any reason to doubt this assessment?

Answer. According to Venezuelan Government-associated media, an estimated 40,000 Cuban advisers and aid workers are in Venezuela, including doctors, teachers, and Cuban military personnel. While both governments have stated that the Cuban presence in Venezuela is limited to these areas, we are also aware of reports of Cuban-Venezuelan cooperation in the intelligence services. We can provide you a more detailed explanation in a classified briefing.

Question. Last year, former Venezuelan intelligence agents and sources with direct access to active officers of the Bolivarian Armed Forces told El Nuevo Herald newspaper that Cuba plays a leading role in the repression unleashed by Maduro against Venezuelan protesters. The Cubans are in charge of operations, which range for security around the Presidential palace to the planning of arrests of opponents.

These Venezuelan sources also told El Nuevo Herald that Cubans have planned the operations of between 600 and 1,000 armed men who comprise the Chavista paramilitary groups, known as "colectivos."

♦ Do you have any reason to doubt this assessment?

Answer. We are aware of media reports indicating that Cuban security and military advisers played a role in activities against Venezuelan protesters, including training pro-government vigilante groups, which subsequently attacked peaceful protesters during demonstrations. However, we have not seen further evidence establishing a direct link between Cuban advisers and these acts of violence. We can provide you a more detailed explanation in a classified briefing.

Question. In 2007, Juan Jose Rabilero, head of Cuba's Committees for the Defense of the Revolution (CDR) claimed that there were over 30,000 members of Cuba's Committees for the Defense of the Revolution in Venezuela.

♦ Do you have any reason to doubt this assessment?

Answer. Cuba and Venezuela have a long-standing and wide-ranging partnership. They cooperate in areas ranging from intelligence services to medical services. We have seen a range of estimates regarding the presence and activities of Cubans in various fields in Venezuela, and are unable to publicly comment on the quality of this information.

Question. According to investigations by independent Venezuelan journalists, the Cubans have computerized Venezuela's public records, giving them control over the issue of identity papers and voter registration. The Cubans have representatives in the ports and airports, and have taken part in the purchases of military equipment. A state-owned Cuban company Albet Ingenieria y Sistemas, received US$170 million to develop electronic data systems in Venezuela. Through Albet, the Cuban Government has been given access to Venezuelan databases, from which it could modify and even issue documents to citizens of other countries. Its portfolio includes the Maduro's communications office, and operating systems for prisons, emergency services, hospitals and police.

♦ Do you have any reason to doubt this assessment?

Answer. Cuba and Venezuela have a long-standing and wide-ranging partnership. They cooperate in areas ranging from intelligence services to medical services. We have seen a range of reports regarding the presence and activities of Cubans in various fields in Venezuela, including the Albet case that you cite. Venezuela is ultimately responsible for the identity documents issued by its agencies.

Question. The Cuban regime has rushed to the side of Venezuela after the administration began to implement the financial sanctions portion of our law. No surprise there given their alliance. But in your normalization talks with Cuba, does the administration categorically rule out putting U.S.-Venezuela policy options on the table, should the regime demand them?

When the President announced his changes to U.S. Cuba policy in December, administration officials touted the changes this would bring to perceptions regarding U.S. policy in the region?

Answer. We have not accepted any preconditions in our talks with the Cuban Government. The current focus of talks with Cuba is on the reestablishment of diplomatic relations and reopening of embassies. Once diplomatic relations are reestablished and embassies reopened, we will be better able to press the Cuban Government on a full range of issues, including human rights, claims, and the return of fugitives from U.S. justice.

The response from partners throughout the region and around the globe to our new approach toward Cuba has been overwhelmingly positive. The updated approach gives us a greater ability to engage other nations in the hemisphere and around the world to join us in promoting respect for human rights and fundamental freedoms in Cuba and throughout the hemisphere.

Question. What has the administration done to rally regional support for U.S. policy toward Venezuela?

Answer. Our policy toward Venezuela reflects our commitment to advance respect for human rights and safeguard democratic institutions, not only in Venezuela, but also across the hemisphere and the world. We have expressed our concerns to governments in the region about the worsening situation in Venezuela. We have urged our partners to speak out in meetings of the Organization of American States and the U.N. Human Rights Council. We have encouraged their support for the release of Mayor Antonio Ledezma, opposition leader Leopoldo Lopez, Mayor Daniel

Ceballos, and others unjustly jailed, including dozens of students, by the Venezuelan Government.

We have also called on regional partners to encourage Venezuela to accept a robust international electoral observation mission, using accepted international standards, for this year's National Assembly elections. We have emphasized to them that the region has an opportunity to play a productive role to support free and fair elections, which will help Venezuela steer toward a democratic solution to tackle its challenges.

We have countered inaccurate claims by the Maduro government and other governments in the hemisphere about the March 9 Executive order and sanctioning of seven individuals and have explained that our actions were within our right to protect U.S. immigration prerogatives and the U.S. financial system. We have stressed that our actions are not against the economy of Venezuela nor the people of Venezuela. We appreciate your remarks on March 17 that helped reinforce this.

We will continue to work closely with others in the region to support greater political expression in Venezuela and to encourage the Venezuelan Government to live up to its shared commitment to democracy and human rights, as articulated in the OAS Charter, the Inter American Democratic Charter, and other relevant instruments.

Question. What regional countries have spoken out against the ongoing human rights abuses in Venezuela?

Answer. The United States is joined by dozens of governments and individuals from the region in calling for the release of Mayor Antonio Ledezma, opposition leader Leopoldo Lopez, Mayor Daniel Ceballos, and others unjustly jailed, including dozens of students, by the Venezuelan Government. These include the Chilean, Colombian, and Peruvian Governments; former Presidents Fernando Henrique Cardoso (Brazil), Sebastian Pinera (Chile), Oscar Arias (Costa Rica), Felipe Calderon (Mexico), Ricardo Martinelli (Panama), Alejandro Toledo (Peru), and Jorge Batlle (Uruguay); and Chilean Senators Isabel Allende, Juan Pablo Letelier, and Ignacio Walker. The Costa Rican Government called for a dialogue between the Venezuelan Government and the opposition and also noted that the OAS should play a role in observing the Venezuelan National Assembly elections. In mourning the death of a student, reportedly at the hands of government forces, OAS Secretary General Jose Miguel Insulza called for ''inclusive dialogue that leads to reconciliation between Venezuelans.''

Question. What regional organizations have done so [spoken out against the ongoing human rights abuses in Venezuela]?

Answer. The OAS Secretary General Jose Miguel Insulza called on the Venezuelan Government to respect the due process of the law in Mayor Antonio Ledezma's case while noting the importance of Venezuela holding National Assembly elections with the ''required democratic character.''

The Inter-American Commission on Human Rights (IACHR) expressed ''deep concern'' on the investigations and prosecutions of Mayor Ledezma, opposition leader Leopoldo Lopez, and Mayor Daniel Ceballos. The body also called on the Venezuelan Government not to criminalize opposition political leaders and to pursue a dialogue with the opposition.

The U.N. High Commissioner for Human Rights (UNHCHR), Zeid Ra'ad Al Hussein, expressed concern over the continued detention of opposition leaders and demonstrators and the government's harsh response to criticism and peaceful expressions of dissent. The European Union (EU) called on the Venezuelan Government to work with the opposition and civil society to meet the legitimate concerns of the Venezuelan people while highlighting that it is important that freedom of expression and fundamental rights are respected in an electoral year. The Canadian, Italian, Norwegian, and Spanish Governments called on the Venezuelan Government to demonstrate its commitment to human rights, including freedom of expression and peaceful protest. Pope Francis urged Venezuelans to refuse violence and called for a sincere and constructive dialogue between the government and the opposition.

On March 14, Union of South American Nations (UNASUR) issued a statement expressing support for a dialogue between all the ''Venezuelan democratic forces'' respecting human rights, rule of law, and institutional order. UNASUR also expressed support for this year's National Assembly elections while emphasizing the importance of respecting the constitutional order and human rights.

Question. Ambassador Brownfield, the Assistant Secretary, Bureau of International Narcotics and Law Enforcement Affairs, has been quoted as saying that recent media reports about the Venezuelan government's complicity with cartels were ''not inconsistent'' with the evidence.

◆ Can you elaborate on Venezuela's interaction with the cartels?
◆ Please describe some of the evidence you have seen that would support this.
◆ What is Cartel de los Soles or the "Cartel of the Suns" relationship with the Venezuelan Government.
◆ Does the Venezuelan Government have a relationship (narcotics trafficking/armed support) with the Revolutionary Armed Forces of Colombia (FARC)? What is the extent of that relationship?

Answer. In Venezuela, public corruption is a major problem that makes it easier for drug-trafficking organizations to move and smuggle illegal drugs, according to Venezuelan nongovernmental organizations. Media reports alleged that some military and law enforcement personnel directly assisted Colombian drug trafficking organizations, including not only the Revolutionary Armed Forces of Colombia (FARC), but also the National Liberation Army (ELN), Clan Usuga, and Los Rastrojos. There are also media reports alleging that Mexican drug-organizations, including the Sinaloa cartel and Los Zetas, operate in Venezuela.

The term "Cartel de los Soles" is used to describe a collection of groups within the Venezuelan Armed Forces that are allegedly involved in drug trafficking. Press reports indicate that elements of the military believed to be most deeply involved in Venezuelan drug trade are concentrated along the western border with Colombia, especially in the states of Apure, Zulia and Tachira.

An indication that some officials at the top level of the military have been involved in drug trafficking are the Treasury Department's designations of current and former Venezuelan Government officials under the Kingpin Act for materially assisting the Revolutionary Armed Forces of Colombia (FARC) in trafficking narcotics. The Venezuelan Government has yet to take action against these government and military officials who have engaged in drug trafficking activities with the FARC.

Question. A recent report by the Washington DC-based, Center for a Secure Free Society, and Canada's Institute for Social and Economic Analysis, raises concerns about the use of Venezuela as a "bridge" to smuggle Iranian agents into North America. It states that Venezuelan authorities provided at least 173 passports, visas, and other documentation—controlled by Cuba's state-owned Albet—to Islamist extremists seeking to slip unnoticed into North America.

◆ Do you have any reason to doubt this assessment?

Answer. We take any allegations that threaten our national security seriously. The Department closely watches all signs of activity of Iranian influence in the Western Hemisphere. We share your concern that Venezuelan citizenship, identity, and travel documents are easy to obtain, making Venezuela a potentially attractive source of documentation for terrorists. International authorities remain suspicious of the integrity of Venezuela documents and their issuance process. We can provide you a more detailed explanation in a classified briefing.

Question. Last month, Nicolas Maduro ordered the arrest of the Mayor of Caracas, Antonio Ledezma, and ordered a further crackdown against student protesters, upon returning from a previously undisclosed trip to Cuba, where Maduro met with both Raul and Fidel Castro.

◆ Do you find the timing curious?

Answer. We have publicly condemned the detention of Caracas Metropolitan Mayor Antonio Ledezma by Venezuelan security forces, as well as the systematic intimidation of other leading opposition figures. It is difficult to speculate on the direct precipitating factors leading to Ledezma's arrest, but the arrest of opposition figures appear to be a clear attempt by the Venezuelan Government to divert attention from the country's economic and political challenges and to destabilize the opposition. Rather than imprisoning and intimidating its critics, the Venezuelan Government should focus on finding real solutions through democratic dialogue.

Venezuela's problems cannot be solved by criminalizing legitimate, democratic dissent. These tactics violate the Venezuelan people's basic human rights and civil liberties as well as the principles and values set forth in the American Declaration of the Rights and Duties of Man and the Inter-American Democratic Charter.

The Venezuelan Government should release those it has unjustly jailed and respect human rights and fundamental freedoms, including the freedoms of expression, association, and peaceful assembly. The United States calls on other countries, leaders, and organizations to urge the Venezuelan Government to cease these efforts to silence the political opposition and further weaken democratic institutions.

Question. What consideration do you give Cuba's continued efforts to subvert democratic institutions in Latin America, including within your review of the State

Sponsors of Terrorism list, on which Cuba was placed in 1982 precisely for its subversive tactics in the Western Hemisphere?

Answer. The Department of State is undertaking a serious review of Cuba's designation based on all relevant, applicable information and the statutory standard. We will not prejudge that process.

Question. Why hasn't the State Department publicly denounced the role that Cuba's Government has played in subverting Venezuela's democratic institutions?

Answer. We should not let the potential influence of outside parties like Cuba distract our attention from the need to hold the Venezuelan Government accountable for its actions. The Venezuelan Government alone is responsible for the actions of its officials and institutions, including those that undermine democracy and the protection of human rights in Venezuela.

The repression and abuses of human rights that occur in Venezuela are the responsibility of the Venezuelan Government.

Question. A July 2009 GAO report (GAO–09–806) stated that the so-called Bolivarian National Guard is deeply involved in the trafficking of illicit narcotics. Please provide an assessment of the Venezuelan National Guard's involvement in illicit trafficking and other transnational criminal activities.

Answer. According to public reports, members of the Bolivarian National Guard continue to facilitate or are directly involved in drug trafficking. Corruption among some members of the Bolivarian National Guard poses a significant threat because of this organization's role in controlling Venezuelan airports, borders and ports. This concern is coupled with the fact that Venezuelan law enforcement does not effectively prosecute drug traffickers, in part due to political corruption.

It is a concern not only for the United States, but also for the rest of the hemisphere, that Venezuela remains a key transit country for the shipment of illegal drugs from South America. The U.S. Government and its regional partners have repeatedly said more effective counternarcotics efforts are necessary to curb the flow of drugs into and out of the region. Since the Venezuelan Government ended formal cooperation with the U.S. Drug Enforcement Agency in 2005, bilateral counternarcotics cooperation has been conducted on a case-by-case basis, including informal information exchanges and maritime interdiction activities with the U.S. Coast Guard. However, a lack of sustained, high-level cooperation reduces the ability of our U.S. law enforcement partners to investigate and prosecute violators of U.S. law residing or operating in Venezuela. We nonetheless encourage our partners to work as closely with their Venezuelan counterparts as is permitted by the Venezuelan Government.

We will continue to support drug interdiction programs throughout the region, including programs in Colombia, Peru, Central America, and the Caribbean. We will urge those partners to encourage the Venezuelan Government to step up its efforts and fulfill regional commitments and responsibilities to combat drug trafficking.